UNDER-GROUND SAINTS

Richard Wurmbrand

▲

PYRAMID BOOKS • NEW YORK

To my children Mikai and Judith and to all those who are working in the service of the "Underground Saints"

UNDERGROUND SAINTS

A PYRAMID BOOK
Published by Pyramid Publications, Inc.,
by arrangement with Fleming H. Revell Company

Pyramid edition published June, 1969

Underground Saints is the U.S. edition of **The Soviet Saints**, published in the United Kingdom by Messrs. Hodder and Stoughton, Ltd.

Translations of articles in the Soviet Press, made by the Library of Congress, are quoted here by permission of the Congress of the United States.

Printed in the United States of America

PYRAMID BOOKS are published by Pyramid Publications, Inc. 444 Madison Avenue, New York, New York 10022, U.S.A.

Courageous, faithful Christians—pictured in this Communist propaganda as despotic and cruel, pale and cunning, fanatic and illiterate—are daily facing exaggerated and twisted evidence for crimes never committed.

Just as they stand unjustly accused by Communists, so may they occasionally appear guilty of certain crimes in the eyes of the civilized world. No blanket standards of morality can be used to judge their actions. The ethical problems they face are almost beyond comprehension.

Let us read in understanding those documented accounts from Soviet newspapers, magazines and courtrooms. Let us remember that in the face of incomprehension, oppression and intolerable circumstances, these UNDERGROUND SAINTS have found the key to eternal happiness—serving Christ whatever the cost.

By the same author

TORTURED FOR CHRIST

Contents

PROLOGUE

CONTENTS

1964

1965

1966

1967

1968

WARNING!!

I publish in this book what I know about the Soviet Saints, together with articles of the Soviet press against them.

I warn the readers that pages 44-180 of the present book contain poisonous anti-Christian propaganda of the Communists who mock the Christians.

The Evangelists considered it necessary to tell us how Jesus was reviled as a gluttonous man, a winebibber, a deceiver and devil. An unmocked truth is not the truth. The Christians of Russia would not be saints if they would not be mocked. The slanders of the Communists against them should be known. Even the mockeries of the Communists serve to show the beauty of the bride of Christ.

Poisons are used by scientists for the production of medicines. Use the poison of the articles of the Soviet press against Christians to stir up in you compassion for those persecuted. Transpose yourself into the situations of those brought before courts, deprived of their children and vilified. "Remember them that are in bonds, as bound with them" (Hebrews 13:3). Understand the Soviet youth who never read any newspapers except those containing such lies against Christianity.

Read the articles of the Soviet press, but be continually on the alert. The Communists lie to you. Seek the beauty of the Underground Church veiled by these mockeries.

I expose here the persecution against believers of all denominations. Christians are on the side of freedom. I, though I have suffered under the Communists, protested publicly when Communists were killed without judgment in Indonesia. Nobody should have to suffer for his convictions, right or wrong. Therefore I publish also the articles about persecution against Witnesses of Jehovah or Old Believers, whom western Christians would not consider as saints.

But not only this. Souls in Russia don't have our privilege of being able to choose from among different denominations and creeds. There are tens of thousands of square miles in which not one single church or Bible is left. To such a spiritually empty place might come a man of any odd sect. Usually he does not know well the teaching of his own sect, but he is the only man to speak out for God and for Christ. Then all the God-seeking people would gather around him.

According to what the founder was, the group would be called—Witnesses of Jehovah, Adventists, or Pentecostals. They would not have been taught any specific doctrine. They simply love Christ and their neighbors, including the Communists who persecute them. Then they have to suffer for their faith. God looks to the heart. In His eyes they are saints.

If you don't like it because they are not Lutherans, Episcopalians, Baptists or Catholics, don't reprove them and don't expel them from the roll of saints. Better ask yourself what you have done to propagate the faith, which you consider as true, behind the Iron Curtain where the darkness of hatred against God reigns.

This book brings you into a world of nightmare. Christians there are jailed, tortured, and have their children taken away. Betrayed by their official leaders, they work underground. In situations apart, you have reactions apart. You cannot judge them according to standards of the free world.

It is alright to turn the other cheek when you yourself are slapped. But what must you do when an informer, infiltrated into the Underground Church by the Communist Secret Police, does not slap you, but betrays hundreds of Christians who will be put in jail, and destroys the possibilities of spreading the Gospel?

Love is not as simple a thing as some believe. Love towards an innocent child, whose life is threatened by a gangster, may oblige a Christian policeman to shoot at the gangster, though he loves every man, gangsters too. When soldiers asked Saint John the Baptist what they should do in order to please God, they were not told to leave the military, but to be righteous in it. Jesus praised highly the faith of a captain in the Roman army. He did not tell him to leave it. As long as there are malefactors, who threaten a country or a civilization from within or without, a church is in danger, as are those of the Underground Church in Russia. A Christian has a duty towards his fellowman, not only to love the malefactor and try to convert him, but also to love those who might become his victims and to defend them—by violence if necessary. This is the dilemma faced by the Underground Church.

The Underground Saints cannot say the whole truth to a Communist interrogator. Don't judge them from the perspective of a free Christian life, but transpose yourself into their positions and understand. Read this book with care!

PROLOGUE

Wearing the Dunce's Cap

Jesus of Nazareth was never under any illusions about what would befall Him. He told His disciples repeatedly that the Son of Man would be given into the hands of men to be mocked and reviled, scourged and crucified. But the beauty of the Son was never more clearly seen than when those very things came to pass.

Epictetus wrote: "It is a kingly thing to do well and to be evil spoken of." This was the lot of Jesus. But the crown of thorns honored Him much more than the ointment used by St. Mary Magdalene when she anointed Him. The blood which flowed from His whipped body clothed him in greater splendor than any robe which His mother, or admiring women, might have woven for Him in earlier days.

Hanging on the cross, He revealed the glory of God much better than when He freely walked through the fields and streets of Palestine.

If we knew nothing about Jesus except what was spoken of Him by His opponents, He would still appear as the most lovable of beings ever to walk of this earth. The Pharisees say to Him: "Master, we know that Thou art true and teachest the way of God in truth" (Matt. 22:16). Pilate declares to the angry crowds: "I am innocent of the blood of this just person" (Matt. 27:24). The man who passed the sentence of death upon Jesus knew Him to be a "just person."

Judas cried: "I have betrayed the innocent blood" (Matt. 27:4). Jesus was innocent even in the mind of the man who betrayed Him.

The crowds who stood at the foot of the cross mocked Him shouting: "He saved others; Himself He cannot save" (Matt. 27:42). Even in their mockery they had to acknowledge that He had in fact "saved others"! In their reviling they uttered one of the greatest truths of the story of salvation. He who had saved others did not save Himself. He who had come down from heaven did not come down from the cross. Because He reduced Himself to weakness, Jesus could redeem sinners.

So it has been throughout the history of mankind. Those

9

rejected by men often prove in the end to be the greatest of men.

Edison was driven out of school at the age of thirteen, written off as an idiot. At the age of fourteen he had already made his first invention. Anatole France's teacher wrote: "This stupid child will never learn to write a good French." But Anatole France became one of the greatest writers of his country, and a member of the French Academy.

Kant was once rejected for a professorship in philosophy. Millet's first paintings were rejected. He was so poor that he could not afford to buy new canvases. His first successful picture, "Oedipus Unbound," was painted over a rejected canvas. The rejection has remained a judgment on his critics.

This familiar story of the rejection of worthy men has been particularly true in the history of the Christian Church. The Inquisition, happily rejected now by our Catholic friends, marched heretics towards the auto-da-fés with dunces' caps on their heads, wearing clothes on which devils in hell-fire were painted. But the faces of the heretics mirrored the beauty of the God for whom they gave their lives. The same applies to those who died for Christ as they have known Him in the Catholic Church.

Those who have discovered that life does not consist in having much, but in being the right thing—a child of God —have appeared most beautiful when they have been most despised.

The story has repeated itself in every generation and it is repeating itself now in Soviet Russia. We present in this book some forty articles collected from the Soviet Press. All these articles speak about Christians of the Underground Church. Orthodox, Baptists, Adventists, Evangelicals, Pentecostals, Old Believers. The Soviet Press mocks them. Once again we see the Christian wearing the dunce's cap of ridicule.

But it is the Communists we pity! They don't know what they do!

When Pilate showed a bleeding, scourged, thorn-crowned Jesus to the Jewish mob and said "Behold the man"—he didn't reveal anything about Jesus. The man he showed was himself! He showed an unrighteous and cruel judge. So it is with the Communists today. In these and many other thousands of articles they revile the Christians, showing them in the most gloomy of colors. But the clearest picture that they give us is not of the Christians, but of themselves. They show their own spiritual darkness. They show how blind they are to the truth and to spiritual beauty.

After reading these articles you will not laugh at the Christians—you will pity their oppressors.

In these articles we see the Christians wearing the dunces' caps—but how beautiful they look in them! Even in the pictures drawn by the Communists, the Bride of Christ appears in her splendor. We see the beauty of those who have turned their backs on material possessions and a life of rest to face trouble and heavy suffering in order that their fellowmen might know eternal life.

While so many Western Christians seem to be engaged in having more comfort, the Christians whom these articles describe are engaged in being something higher. A letter received from the Underground Church in the Communist camp says: "We don't wish to be better Christians. It is wrong to have this desire. We wish to be the only kind of Christians that Christ meant us to be: Christlike Christians." Certainly, as you read about Christians in the Soviet Union, even as they are described by their worst enemies, by their torturers and by murderers, you have the impression that you are meeting with Christ Himself. Here is Christ's mystical body, the real Church, which is ready to suffer as her Master for the glory of God and the good of mankind.

Observations

Before we proceed to read the articles themselves, there are a number of things that I want to explain. The Western reader may well pass by phrases in these press reports that are full of significance.

In this section, therefore, I propose to pick out several issues from the articles and comment on them in the light of my own experiences as one of the leaders of the Underground Church in Rumania.

Fishers of Men

"Baptists ... attempt to catch in their nets as many victims as possible" (Article 4, p. 61).

How true is this in the Communist camp? For several

years I led the secret missionary work in the Soviet Army. I have never met a single lukewarm Russian Christian. In the West, Christians swim in Bibles and other forms of religious literature, yet they are often slothful in giving them to others. With us, Christian literature is printed on secret printing presses and is very scarce. Very often it has to be written by hand—even in the case of Bibles and New Testaments! But, oh, how zealous the Christians are to give out this literature! The Soviet newspapers say that even children in school put handwritten Christian leaflets in the pockets of their teachers' overcoats.

These Christians I speak of really believe that any man they encounter is an eternal soul. They feel that they cannot be indifferent towards the people they meet, for their eternal destiny depends on knowing spiritual truth. So they try to open men's eyes.

I remember in Rumania that I only had to sit quietly in my home, and things would happen. One after another, members of my Underground Church would appear with some new soul they had "caught in their net," perhaps as the result of a chance meeting in the queue for bread or potatoes. Perhaps a man would bring someone from his factory whose interest had been awakened. Often Christians would enter "pubs" to find souls.

I have never known an inactive Christian. There is no such person, for a Christian is either active for God or he is active for the devil. With us they were active for God.

Even when Christians were put in prison their zeal to win souls for Christ continued. In solitary confinement they learned to tap the Gospel in morse code against their cell walls. They witnessed to their jailors who had whips in their hands.

Sometimes we "caught in our nets" very big fish! Gheorghiu-Dej, the former Prime Minister of Rumania, was won for Christ by a servant-maid in his house just as, centuries ago, the servant-maid St. Sophia had won over Empress Helena, mother of Constantine the Great. The Empress, in turn, had convinced her son to give liberty to the Christians in the Roman Empire, and this changed the history of the Christian Church and the history of the world. The Underground Church has penetrated behind the walls of the Kremlin itself. The daughter of the greatest mass-murderer of Christians was won for God. Brought up under the strictest Communist discipline, Svetlana Stalin is a trophy of grace.

I have seen Christians in Communist prisons who were dying and yet witnessing until their last breath.

Submission to Christ

"Baptists ... undermine their will power" (Article 4, p. 61). This is the Communists' way of saying that Christians teach men to submit their wills to the will of God. What a great achievement this is!

I remember when I was first harassed under the Communists in 1948. Along with others I was put in terrible conditions. We were in solitary confinement and our cells were guarded by big dogs. When we went to the toilet or to the bath we were escorted by guards with revolvers in their hands.

I was scared. I cannot pretend to pose as a hero. I was a simple man and sometimes, in my misery, I felt I could not say our Lord's Prayer. When I came to the words "Thy will be done" I would stop. I found myself saying: "Father, Thy will be done in all matters, but in one matter I must ask my will and not Thine. Take me out of these terrible circumstances. I cannot bear them any longer!"

I remember the happiness that came to me when, after an agonizing spiritual struggle, I could say to God: "Thy will be done in this matter also. If you wish me here, I will do my best for Thy Glory even in a dungeon." And God rewarded me richly. I was able to witness to Christ before my interrogator and he was deeply impressed.

We can only congratulate the Russian Christians for "undermining the will power of their fellow men" in this sense.

Avoiding Communist Propaganda

"The Leaders of the sect teach their flock; do not attend movies or theatres ... do not sing, except pious songs" (Article 4, p. 61).

Every Russian film is a vehicle of propaganda, spreading an ideology of hatred and Godlessness. The Christian leaders are right to warn their flocks of such influences.

When the Communists came to power in Rumania they put their propaganda posters everywhere—even in street-cars and busses. Their posters showed the crimes of earlier regimes and demanded that the former rulers of our country should be hanged. The posters contained terrible pictures of actual hangings. My son was only five years old at the time and I can remember him traveling in a streetcar with his hands over his eyes. "I don't wish even to see these ugly things," he said. He had the right Christian instinct.

I cannot help comparing this teaching of Russian Underground Church leaders about godless movies and pious songs with what I see in the West, even in Christian families. There are even families of Christian pastors who will spend evening after evening in front of their television sets. And all the dirt of some of those television shows is gloated upon without discrimination. The warnings about dirty sex films are rarely heard.

When the Communists reproach the Russian Christian leaders for teaching discrimination in these matters, they say something that reflects nothing but credit.

Caring for the Weak

"The Leaders of the Baptist sect pay special attention to people who find themselves in a difficult situation or plight, and to inexperienced boys and girls" (Article 4, p. 61).

I have been an "inexperienced boy" in a capitalistic country, and I have passed through many "difficult situations." It was not until I was twenty-seven that I met a Christian who would stop me on the street and speak about the way of salvation. And this was not a pastor but a carpenter. What should a priest or pastor be doing?

When I was fourteen a friend took me to a brothel for the first time. In Bucharest there was a quarter of the town filled with pubs, gambling houses and other houses of perdition. I became a regular customer of those places.

Not once did I meet a pastor near the doors of such a place warning young people to keep clear!

Now Communism has taught Christians to become earnest and to value souls. Jesus left heaven and descended into hell for souls, and he would have done it if there had been only one soul to save. The Russian Christians seek out those inexperienced boys and girls in difficult situations and show them the truth. So says the Russian Press. Another compliment to the Christians from their worst enemies!

The pastors of the Underground Church don't teach doctrine to their young people. Being untrained they know little enough themselves. But then—what is doctrine? It is the storehouse of past experiences. These persecuted Christians have the actual experience of the cross and of its victory in their daily lives.

Not often the pastors try to win the youth with logical arguments which seldom convince. Rather they exhale the love of Christ. It is by this love that young people are being won.

It is indeed true that "the leaders of the Baptist sect pay special attention to people who find themselves in a difficult situation or plight."

In the Communist countries, many people are in great need. The Communists may propagate a doctrine of equality, but while their leaders live in luxury, the simple worker or farmer who is a party worker is very little cared for. In Russia the real community of goods is practiced by the Christians rather than the Communists. In the Underground Church you will find the same sort of situation that is described in the Bible—"they had all things common ... distribution was made unto every man according as he had need" (Acts 4:32, 35).

Not surprisingly, the Lord adds to their number "daily" (Acts 2:47).

Violence in the Church

The Soviet Union is a member of the so-called United Nations Organization and has signed the declaration of the rights of man. Among other things, this declaration assures to everyone full religious liberty.

Now, however, we see them saying in their newspaper that "Some people looking around like thieves, are sneaking along Kirov Street toward house No. 44" (Article 4, p. 61). Why must these people have to sneak like thieves? Have they bad things in mind? No—the Communist newspaper tells us the reason. They are going to a secret prayer meeting. And why does a prayer meeting have to be secret?

Because prayer meetings are forbidden. They have to be held underground! So much for "religious liberty"!

Now—so the Communist paper tells us—at one of these prayer meetings something unusual has happened. The Christians have beaten up one of their number with the name of Valerii (Article 4, p. 61). Why should Christians do such a thing?

Not that the Communists have any scruples over beating and torturing their fellow men; they have been doing it for fifty years! They make no secret of this. Marx, Lenin,

Stalin, Kosygin and Mao Tse-Tung have terror as one of
the essential points in their teaching. Beating is justifiable
when it is done by themselves, but unjustifiable when it is
done by Christians.

How is it that such a thing could be reported as having
happened among Christians? It is because the secret police
infiltrate the Underground Church. By blackmail, bribery
and threats they transform some of the believers into
"squealers" and informers prepared to denounce their
brethren. Now the disciples of Jesus know how to be meek,
but they remember that a whip was also a tool in the hands
of their Master. They know that the highest Christian
virtue is not love in the sentimental sense but in a balanced
sense. The truly loving attitude knows when to be humble
and when to be self-asserting; when to be submissive and
when to be harsh.

Violence is one of the many rights of Christians. Christians in the Underground Church cannot allow informers to
wreak havoc and expose the brethren to the possibilities of
arrest and torture. So informers in Russia are beaten—and
sometimes Christians may go further than this. When one
of the articles accuses Christians of attempting to kill
someone—it may not have been entirely an invention
(Article 4, p. 61). The traitors must know that their own
lives are in jeopardy if they betray. Christians in the
Communist camp are in a war, and the officers of Christ's
army have to care for the safety of their soldiers.

No pity should be shown to the sworn enemies of
Christianity while they do harm to the churches. Let us be
wise in the kind of compassion we show. King Saul was a
Stalin of his time and David spared his life twice. Was
David right in this unlimited kindness? I don't agree with
sparing the life of a man like Saul who put a whole city to
the sword, "men and women, children and sucklings, and
oxen, and asses, and sheep" (I Sam. 22:19). I admire
rather Cromwell, who finished with a tyrant.

It is said of St. Francis of Assisi that he once came
across a wolf when he was walking through a wood in the
company of other friars. At once his brother friars wanted
to shoot the beast. "Don't shoot brother wolf," said the
famous Saint. "He also is a creature of God." This, of
course, was all very well for St. Francis, who, reputedly,
could tame the wildest animal. Generally speaking, however, I would feel it only right to spare a wolf if this

guaranteed that he would not eat his "sister" sheep. Should this danger persist, then I, as a shepherd, am obliged, by my love for the sheep, to kill the wolf!

Only a rigid attitude toward informers can make it possible for us to continue with underground meetings, secret printing presses and secret literature distribution.

If the Communists want to put us in the dunce's cap for this, and call us beaters and killers—then we shall wear it unashamedly.

Under Observation

Are the Communists watching? The answer is "yes" and "no"! The Communists are men, and therefore they are as much God's creatures as Christians. Tertullian refers to the soul as naturally Christian, and thus he refers to oppressors and torturers, too. Nobody is a wholehearted Communist. The Communists are divided souls. Colonel Penkovski, one of the heads of the Russian Secret Police, shot by his comrades for the services he rendered to the cause of freedom, wrote in his memoirs that he was praying before ever he came into contact with Christians in the West.

Many of the Communists—even officers of the Secret Police—detest the Godless attitude of their party and their rulers. They "turn a blind eye" to the secret activities of Christians.

Again and again in Communist newspapers we find the complaint that whereas the Christians are zealous, the atheists are inactive. It is because truth burns like a fire—it is always united with zeal. The Communists are, in fact, very doubtful about themselves and about their doctrines. Their unsureness makes them slothful, and sometimes complacent toward Christians. High-ranking Communists with divided souls made my coming to the West possible. Such men helped Svetlana Stalin to defect.

In High Places

"The father of the Communist, Peter Grechikhin, the Secretary of the Komgomol of the Center of Technical Inspection of the Ush Tobe station is the head of the Baptist community. Peter's wife is also a sectarian" (Article 4, p. 61).

As I read these words I know that there is more to it than that! Often secretaries of the Communist Youth Association are themselves hidden Christians as well as their relatives. Peter's father is one of the hundreds of thousands of hidden Christians in Russia. In Jesus' time we read of Joseph of Arimathea, the disciple who hid his discipleship. There was a time in the history of Israel when Elijah the prophet thought himself to be the only one on the side of God. But God knew that there were 7,000 others. These others had hidden their faith but they had not lost it.

God understands human weakness. God forgives this bargaining with conscience. For us it is important to know that in Russia there exist vast numbers of people who believe in Christ, but who retain positions in Communist organizations. When the right time comes they will be on our side in the fight against the powers of Godlessness.

Stars Fall

The Communist papers report several cases where pastors and priests have recanted. They are no surprise to us. Christ Himself said: "He that received the seed into stony places, the same is he that heareth the word, and anon with joy receiveth it; yet hath he not root in himself, but dureth for a while: for when tribulation or persecution ariseth because of the word, by and by he is offended" (Matt. 13:20-21). I have seen terrible treachery from those of whom you would least expect it.

Jesus told us that one of the signs of the end of time would be the falling of the stars. As there are movie stars, so we have stars in the religious world. Some of these stars enjoy shining for their own sake, and when they cannot shine any more by preaching Christianity they choose to shine by teaching Communism. In Rumania there were three great Christian poets. Now their poetry is in honor of the Bolshevik rulers.

When the priests of the chosen people stood mocking at the foot of the cross, God ordained on the spot a priest from a robber who witnessed to the truth and called his fellow criminal to repent. Today in the Communist camp God is continuing this ordination of the most unlikely of people. While some preachers and priests leave their faith, Communists are converted. The Soviet papers say it!

Some young Communists tear off their red scarves and publicly attest to their faith in baptism. Others remain within the ranks of the Communist party. They appear to be Godless, but in fact they work for the protection of the Underground Church.

The program of the Communist Party of the Soviet Union states: "Religious beliefs came into being in the past on the basis of the domination of the elementary forces of nature over the people, and social oppression." Today the Soviet papers bear witness to the fact that religious beliefs also came into being under the domination of the Communists—even within the ranks of the party itself!

Transparent Lies

To lie is a difficult art. There exists no perfect liar just as there exists no perfect criminal. Liars as well as criminals have consciences that play them tricks. Just at the crucial moment criminals always make mistakes. They leave the vital clue behind which helps the police to track them down. At the moment of committing the crime there is something in their hearts condemning the very deed they commit.

It is the same with liars. We have been created by God for the truth. This makes the Communist lies appear so stupid that nobody can believe them any more.

For example, *Kazakhstanskaia Pravda* carried a report of a criminal trial against the leaders of an illegal Baptist community. The charge was that they had obliged their children to pray by threatening to put them in chains or even to death (Article 12, p. 83).

Now we all know Baptists. Such things do not happen in a Baptist house!

Once again the dunce's cap has been put on the head of Christians. What is in fact true is that Christians have a very geat concern for the salvation of their children. They pray much for them and they teach them to pray.

Some thirty years ago I stayed in the home of a Rumanian General and his wife. The wife was a very earnest Christian, but her son lived a careless and licentious life. She asked me to pray for him, and I did thereafter. So did many other Christians. Years later in prison I met the son myself. He had become a Colonel in the army and then the Communists had sentenced him to life imprisonment. At first I didn't know who he was. I witnessed to him for the Lord and he was converted. It was then that I learned that he was the one for whom his mother, I and many others had been praying.

It is prayer that wins the children of Christians, not chains! The lie of the Communists is too gross to be believed.

Mentally Retarded

In *Uchitelskaia Gazeta* (Teacher's Gazette) the Communists say that usually the children of Christians are poor students and mentally retarded (Article 21, p. 113).

We must be patient with men! It is useless to ask for a fig in the winter—you have to wait for the following autumn. So it is with the Communists. They are the ones who are backward, and we cannot expect much clear thinking from them. How incredible that the Communists can connect Christian faith with mental poverty!

When Michael Faraday, the world-famous English physicist, lay on his deathbed a colleague asked him: "Faraday, what are your speculations now?"

"Speculations!" replied the dying scientist. "I have none. Thank God I am not resting my dying head on speculations. I know whom I have believed and am sure that He is able to keep that which I have committed unto Him against that day." Was *he* mentally underdeveloped?

Lord Kelvin has been another of the world's greatest physicists. He said: "If you think strongly enough, you will be forced by science to believe in God." For him, belief was the product of strong thought, not of mental backwardness. Why this unkind connection of mental underdevelopment with Christian belief?

Was Francis Bacon, the English philosopher and statesman, mentally poor? He said: "A little philosophy inclineth man's mind to atheism; but depth in philosophy bringeth men's minds about to religion." Religion makes our children think more deeply. Usually Christian children are above the average of pupils.

We could give innumerable quotations from the greatest men of science who expressed their faith in God. Sir James Jeans said: "Our universe seems to be more like a great thought than a great machine. I would say as a speculation, not as a scientific fact, that the universe is a creation of some great universal mind underlying and co-ordinating all our minds . . . scientific thought seems to be moving in that direction."

It has never been harmful to any child to be taught about religion. Religion broadens the mind and gives depth to thought. It must, however, be noted that these claims of *Uchitelskaia Gazeta* are in fact contradicted by statements in other Soviet papers. *Kazakhstanskaia Pravda* describes Christian students as "exemplary," and *Komsomolskaia Pravda* writes: "We usually imagine our ideological foes . . . as mentally retarded. . . . But Shevchenko is an engineer by education, strong, smart and diabolically shrewd" (Article 13, p. 86).

Christians as Thieves

What an ugly dunce's cap is put on the head of the Christian Ian Pinka (Article 20, p. 108). He has spent, we are told, five years in prison for robbery. I can well believe it for I know what is qualified as "robbery" in a Communist country.

The Red Government has collectivized the agriculture. They have taken away from the individual farmers their right to possess their fields, vineyards and cattle. To take a sheaf of wheat or a few grapes from what were formerly your own fields or vineyards is qualified as theft. If a barber takes a razor out of his former barber's shop—he is a thief!

The offerings taken in the official churches cannot be administered independently by the pastor or priest. No expense can be made without the approval of the Communist Ministry of Cults, which does not allow any charitable work or repairs to buildings and obliges the pastors to receive minimal salaries so that they live near starvation level. Many pastors and priests do not comply with such regulations. But if they are caught using church money for church purposes without the approval of the atheist Ministry of Cults, they go to prison for theft!

The Christians thus in prison for theft are forced to wear a very ugly dunce's cap—but, then, it is better to be falsely accused of being a thief than to be falsely honored for a good deed!

It must have been heartrending for our brother Pinka to hear his father disowning him before the Court. But the father had to do it or else he would probably have lost his job and even gone to prison also. Had the father also been imprisoned, who would have looked after Pinka's children? Perhaps also it was in the mind of Pinka's father to continue the underground work left by Pinka on his imprisonment. These are the dramas and dilemmas of the

Soviet saints. I have seen a Christian dying of a heart attack in Rumania while he told his fellow prisoners how his own daughter had witnessed against him in Court because otherwise her little children would have become motherless.

Breaking the Law

The Russian Christians are again and again accused of breaking the Soviet Laws and of not being obedient to the State. These charges are true.

Is it right to break laws? Even Western Christians tell us sometimes that the Underground Church does wrong by not obeying the laws of the country, and they remind us to render to Caesar what is Caesar's and "Let every soul be subject unto the higher powers" (Rom. 13:1).

What is the Russian Christians' answer to this?

First of all, there are times when even the ten commandments of God lose their rights. "When he was an hungred," saith Jesus (Matt. 12:3), David did what was forbidden by law. Hunger cares little about laws. When your country is invaded or oppressed by tyrants, you have to defend it, and the commandment "Do not kill" does not apply. Still less have we necessarily to obey every merely manmade law.

Render to Caesar what is Caesar's? Now, let us be reasonable and establish first what was Caesar's in Palestine at that time? Just nothing. The Romans were able to seize Palestine because they were strong and the Jews were a small nation. Nothing was theirs in Palestine. The houses had been constructed by the Jews. The trees had been planted by Jews. Even the crosses on which Jews were nailed were made by Jewish carpenters. The Romans had as many rights in Palestine as the Russians have in Hungary or Rumania. And as to Caesar, nothing was his even in Rome. Julius Caesar had been a general of the Roman Republic which was over 400 years old. He overthrew the Republic and became dictator. He was followed by a dynasty, of which most were madmen and sadists, such as Nero, Claudius or Caligula.

If you were to say to a Hungarian today, "Give to the Russians what belongs to the Russians" he could only interpret this as "Give them a good kick in the back and drive them out of the country." This is surely what any Jew understood when Jesus said "Render therefore unto

Caesar the things which are Caesar's" (Matt. 22:21). It is a revolutionary word and not one which teaches us to be bootlickers of transitory tyrants. And then supposing that it meant that we have to be submissive to any king under any circumstances, or to any legitimate ruler; this word would implicitly forbid us to be submissive to those who overthrow the legitimate government. The Caesar of Russia was a member of the Romanov dynasty. All citizens of Russia pledged allegiance when they entered the army. What allegiance did they owe to the Bolsheviks who shot in cold blood not only the Czar but also his family, including a small sick boy, his heir? What allegiance did the Rumanians owe to the Communist Government which, without asking the people, drove out of the country our "Caesar," King Michael the First?

Supposing that Hitler had invaded Great Britain and made his headquarters in Buckingham Palace; would British Christians have had to be on his side or on the side of their own king? Asking this question implies its answer. Thus, render to Caesar what is Caesar's means to be against the Communist rulers.

The verses following "Let every soul be subject unto the higher powers" (Rom. 13) explain who these higher powers are. They are those who reward good and punish evil. If rulers reward evil and punish good, they are not ordained by God. Their laws are worth just nothing. Christians choose, in such a case, to obey God rather than men.

Jefferson has said, "Resistance to tyranny is obedience to God."

Children Separated from Parents

Ianis and Zenta Osma have been stripped of their parental rights because they taught their children Christianity. Their children have been handed over to the State for their upbringing. In Court, the last words of the father were: "I am exchanging children for God" (Article 21, p. 113).

For fourteen years I was in a Communist jail, separated from my children. The grief was unspeakable. During winter days we pressed our naked breasts toward the icy iron bars to quench the fire of longing which burned on in our hearts. During the night you would hear the prisoners whispering the names of their children as they dreamed.

Thousands of children have been taken away from their

parents in Communist countries for one "crime"—their parents taught them about Christ.

It is told that when Alexander the Great was a child, he once visited a sculptor and found the man's studio full of statues. His sight was drawn to one that had its head covered and bore wings on its feet. When he asked for the name of the statue the sculptor told him that it represented the "Image of Opportunity."

"But why cover the face?" asked the young Alexander.

"Because men rarely see the opportunity when it passes in front of them!"

"But why does it have wings on its feet?" asked the young king.

"Because once it flies by," said the sculptor, "opportunity is gone forever."

The Communists have exceptional opportunities before them in these Christian children. Simeon in the Temple saw a child and his spiritually awakened eyes recognized the boy Jesus as the Savior of the world. The Communists have before them miracles of innocence, grace and self-sacrifice. They have care of children who are witnessing to their faith at the greatest cost that can be asked of a child. We can only pray that, like Simeon of old, their eyes may see more than just these small human beings. At present they have no eyes to see the shining faces of these children or the angels who encamp around them.

In Russia today there are children who die as heroes of their faith. Others witness to Christ even in the atheistic boarding schools where they have been forcibly sent. Some, but very few, yield under threatenings and beatings and deny their parents before Court.

Under the emotional stress of arrest, small children have signed blank sheets of paper on which the Communist authorities later wrote: "We wish to be taken away from our parents." The children were threatened with rearrest if they would not stand by their declarations. Tragedies like this lie behind the article "Six who made the choice" (Article 17, p. 98). The mother said before the Court one phrase only: "I am suffering for my faith."

An old Egyptian legend tells how God created fish, animals and birds from clay. Then he wished to create man. When he put his hand in the mud for this purpose, a crab bit him. A few drops of blood flowed out and mixed with the clay. God is supposed to have said: "This clay has been sanctified with my blood and is too good for making man. We will use it to make mother-hearts."

There is nothing more tender than mother-hearts, but the Communists are treading upon them ruthlessly in these days.

Child Murder?

You will read, probably with horror, of the Christian Anna (Article 7, p. 75). She preferred to throw both herself and her child under a train, and to explain to the all-understanding Jesus why she had done so. Anna was horrified at the thought of her child being changed in an atheistic boarding school into someone who could become a ruthless persecutor of Christians. So she decided to kill both the child and herself. Her circumstances were maddening.

I have been in maddening circumstances and I know what can be their outcome. I have never been a madman. A madman is one who has abnormal reactions. I had the normal reactions of a man put in abnormal situations. If a man were to shriek continually this would be a sign of madness. But if a man were to endure hours of physical tortures, then shrieking would be a normal reaction. When one encounters great mental stress it is not always easy to distinguish between normal reactions to maddening circumstances and attitudes of craziness.

Mrs. Rykova had her son and daughter taken from her. Try being separated from your children for just one week without any news from them—then you will know how it is! Her crime was her explosive temperament. She tore off her son's red uniform scarf and forbade her daughter, Lyuba, to wear the insignia of the Soviet children (Article 34, p. 176).

Her temperament led her to much worse. When her brethren in the faith, the Mitichkin family, ignored her advice and accepted a loan of 300 roubles from the State bank to buy a cow, Mrs. Rykova treated this as an act of cooperation with Antichrist. Considering these parents to be traitors to the faith, she killed their son, Valery, for whom she cared. To her Valery was better dead than to be growing up as a child of Judas and a son of hell.

This is a terrible thing to record. But who are you to judge? No blanket standards of morality can be employed here. Do you know how a mother feels when two children

are taken away from her by Godless rulers? Do you know
how you would react?

I chose just a few examples out of hundreds of documents. I think of a woman who attempted to kill her
daughter. The girl had become an informer against the
brethren. She had been corrupted by the Secret Police.
Men had been put in prison because of her. I myself have
met Christian mothers who have told me the tragic stories
of their girls brought to such debasement. The grief of
those mothers far surpassed the grief of mothers who had
children in prison for Christ's sake.

We walk on holy ground here. We read new pages of the
Old Testament. We have to keep silent.

Remember this: It is clear from the documents we
present that the Communists admit to forcibly taking
children from Christian parents if those parents can be
shown to be sharing their faith with their children. Those
children are taken to atheistic boarding schools and
brought up in a godless manner. The intolerable circumstances are of the Communists' own making and therefore
all that follows, even the crimes, must be set against the
Communists, not against those who feel driven into horrible
reaction.

Abraham lied about his wife Sarah when they dwelt in
Egypt. He claimed that she was only his sister (Gen. 12).
Pharaoh, not realizing that Sarah was Abraham's wife,
took her into his house. We read that God plagued Pharaoh
for this, rather than Abraham who was the liar. Why was
this? It was because Pharaoh had cruel laws whereby a
foreigner who had a beautiful wife could be killed and the
wife taken to become the King's mistress. Identical situations are described in Genesis, chapter 26, where the King
of Gerar is involved. The sin was not Abraham's but the
King's. Abraham lied for self-protection and for the sake
of his little sect of monotheists. It might even be called not
a "lie," but a "stratagem."

Western Christians will find it difficult to understand
what Anna Bavalennaia and Maria Rykova did. We must
try to see the tempest in the hearts of these mothers. They
thought that their children would be eternally lost because
of Communist indoctrination. There are no liberals and
modernists in Russian theology. Christians there believe in
a hell for all unbelievers.

These mothers knew the story of Joseph Stalin. He was

the son of a godly mother whose dying words to her son had been: "How sorry I am that you did not become a priest!" He had been destined for the priesthood, but Marxism made the possible priest into a mass murderer. Anna's child would have had to learn the same poisonous Marxism.

When my wife and I were both arrested, my son was left on the streets with no family and no prospects of any education other than atheistic. You may think badly of me for saying this, but I prayed that he would rather die than become Godless. I have known many other imprisoned Christians to pray as I did. I understand Anna and Rykova.

Suicide

Anna attempted suicide. When I was in prison I also prepared to take my life in case I might prove unable to stand up to my tortures. I said to myself: "It is better to kill myself than to get to the point where I betray the brethren. I will go to Jesus and explain why I took my own life. He will surely understand."

The problem of suicide under exceptional circumstances is not a settled one in Christian ethics. Hamlet said that the Everlasting had "fixed His cannon 'gainst self-slaughter"—but, then, Hamlet was no theologian!

Among the theologians, even St. Augustine vacillates in this matter. In *The City of God* he writes on the one hand: "It is not without significance that in no passage of the holy canonical books there can be found either divine precept or permission to take away our own life ... for the sake of ... ridding ourselves of anything whatever. Nay, the law, rightly interpreted, even prohibits suicide, where it says 'Thou shalt not kill.' This is proved specially by the omission of the words 'thy neighbor,' which are inserted when false witness is forbidden: 'Thou shalt bear no false witness against thy neighbor.' "

The problem is important for him because many Christian girls had committed suicide during the Roman persecution to avoid being put in brothels, a punishment used by the tyrants of those days.

He admits therefore: "They who have laid violent hands on themselves are perhaps to be admired for their greatness of soul, though they cannot be applauded for the soundness of their judgment. However, if you look at the matter more closely, you will scarcely call it greatness of soul which prompts a man to kill himself rather than bear up against some hardships of fortune or sins in which he is not implicated.... Saintly Job endured dreadful evils in his body rather than deliver himself from all torment by self-inflicted death.... At all events, if it be true, as the truth plainly declares, that suicide is a detestable and damnable wickedness, who is such a fool as to say: Let us sin now, that we may obviate a possible future sin; let us now commit murder, lest we perhaps afterwards should commit adultery? Is it not better to commit a wickedness which penitence may heal, than a crime which leaves no place for healing contrition?"

But on the other hand Augustine praises Samson for having taken his own life. He considers him justified in so doing, because "the Spirit ... had given him secret instructions to do this." He also writes: "They say, in the time of persecution some holy women escaped those who menaced them with outrage, by casting themselves into rivers, which they knew would drown them; and, having died in this manner, they are venerated in the Catholic church as martyrs. Of such persons I do not presume to speak rashly. I cannot tell whether there may not have been vouchsafed to the church some divine authority, proved by trustworthy evidences, for so honoring their memory. It may be that it is so. It may be they were not deceived by human judgment, but prompted by divine wisdom, to their act of self-destruction. We know that this was the case with Samson. And when God enjoins any act, and intimates by plain evidence that He has enjoined it, who will call obedience criminal? Who will accuse so religious a submission ... ? He who knows that it is unlawful to kill himself, may nevertheless do so if he is ordered by Him whose commands we may not neglect."

Scripture says: "For what man knoweth the things of a man, save the spirit of man which is in him?" (I Cor. 2:11).

Anna, the suicide, may be a crowned saint in heaven now. Many took their own lives in Rumanian prisons, too. Recently a man who has helped most the Underground Church in Rumania committed suicide, after having been in prison twice.

You don't know Anna's grief for her child. Don't judge.

Perhaps what I have said about this matter is already too much. The writer to the Hebrews was very wise when he wrote "... time would fail me to tell of ... Samson."

About many things it is better that nothing be said. Those who look for an opportunity to take offense are many. We must be careful not to say more than an unbelieving age is able to bear.

Miraculous Healings

Some of the Christians referred to in the documents we present are in prison for the crime of "miraculous healings." According to the Communist authorities, such things are impossible!

However, I myself was sick in prison with lung, spinal and intestinal tuberculosis and recurring jaundice. The "medicines" I received were beatings, neglect and lack of food. Doctors in Oslo who later examined me and took X-rays could not believe at first that I had survived the Rumanian prison conditions, with four vertebrae infected with tuberculosis, lungs like sieves, and without food and drugs. The healing virtue of Christ had proved to be the same as in the times of the Gospel. Today He delivers many of the fighters of the Underground Church from their infirmities through the prayers of the faithful.

We read in the *Journal of George Fox,* the founder of the Quakers, that when he was released from the prison in Newcastle he could heal. So can many who have passed through Communist jails.

The Communists may mock such healings as fakes— again they put the dunce's caps on our heads! But I know that I was mortally sick and I know that I am now very much alive! Thousands can tell the same story.

In September 1967 the London *Church Times* published an open letter to the Soviet leaders of a Christian called Krawchenko. In it one could read of a member of the Russian Underground Church who had been so ill in prison because of cancer that the authorities released him knowing death was imminent. God kept that man alive to tell, with courage, the truth about the persecution.

The Good Effects of Persecution

Jesus once said: "Beware ye of the leaven of the Pharisees, which is hypocrisy" (Luke 12: 1). We must frankly admit that hypocrisy appears in Christian fellowships far too often. It appears particularly where Christians are free and considered by society to be "respectable."

Here the prayers are often from the lips but not from the hearts.

Communism has stamped out many things—including hypocrisy among Christians. Nobody earns anything other than trouble and suffering by being religious, or a faithful Church leader. The whole quality of religious life has been changed by this. Diamonds are nothing but black coal put under very heavy pressure. Under the pressure of Communism, the Christians have become beautiful gems!

Ecstasy

Living under pressure has also changed their manner of praying. In another issue of *Kazakhstanskaia Pravda* we read that the Christians when they pray "get into ecstasy" (Article 4). How happy I would be if the same were true of Western Christians also!

"Glory be to God on high" sang the angels on the first Christmas Eve. You cannot truly give glory in the lower spheres. The Greek word for "holy" is *hagios* which means etymologically—"unearthly." "Hallowed be Thy name" means, literally translated: "May Thy name be risen above the earthly spheres." Prayer that allows a man's mind to remain in the spheres below is blasphemous prayer. It tears God down from His exalted place. We must ascend in prayer rather than make God descend.

"Ecstasies"—which means in the Greek "to be out of yourself"—implies that you are somewhere other than in your usual state of mind. To be truly ascended in the heavenly places should be the normal state of the Christian's soul during prayer. The prayers of the first Christians were ecstatic, so also the prayers of God's saints through all times. This is now a current happening in the Communist camp. Sufferings have purified the hearts of God's people and their prayers are transformed. The Communists call them "obscurantists" and "monsters" for this. They bring out the dunce's caps again—but the heads are surrounded by halos of holiness.

Ecstasy is very little known in the West now. The Western Christian has the television. The word "television" means "to see far" but just because of his television he doesn't in fact see very far at all! He sees only a golf tournament from somewhere nearby. In the Underground Church we have a television set recommended by Jesus

Himself: "Blessed are the pure in heart: for they shall see God" (Matt. 5:8).

In secret meetings in basements and attics, or in solitary-confinement cells, we knew the ecstasy.

We began with meditation, remembering how many "houses" had held our lives in the past: the tiny body of the baby, the small frame of the child, the full flesh of the adolescent and mature man. We reflected on how our lives had become contained in broken vessels and decaying bodies. But all these bodies that had clothed us were only "houses." Life is an entity in itself beyond these "houses." And we discovered that entity.

We had known humiliations and victories. We had known clean thoughts and unclean thoughts. We had known sins, and deeds of righteousness. But outside and beyond all these things we saw the Builder of the tabernacle of the body. We saw the Lord of the soul. He is within ourselves—hidden deep—the Lord who "said that he would dwell in the thick darkness" (I Kings 8:12).

And when you discover Him, the eternal jewel within yourself, even walls of prison cells shine like diamonds. Gone are the deceits and delusions. You are delivered from bonds. The bride is in the arms of the heavenly Bridegroom, and you forget! You receive the kiss which is the subject of the Song of Songs. While lips are kissed, one cannot speak any more! You have passed from the sphere of words to the sphere of reality.

No notion about God is God. No doctrine, no thought about God is God. The word of God is not God. Our love to God is not God. In ecstasy you pass from the sphere of words. You pass from the sphere of false thoughts but also from the sphere of true thoughts. You pass from the sphere of false doctrines but also from the sphere of true doctrines. You pass from the sphere of sins but also from the sphere of righteous acts. You pass into the realms of reality. God has cleansed you. He has illuminated you and now you are united with Him. It is the marriage of the soul with Christ.

The Communists mock this experience. They adorn the bride and the bridegroom with a dunce's cap. But what does it matter to a bride and to a bridegroom, when they are madly in love, what others think and say about them? They have forgotten that the world even exists. She is His and He is hers: "He feedeth among the lilies" (Song of Solomon).

Sovetskaia Justitsia puts this matter better than Western theological professors: "The role of the sectarian preachers ... is carrying the process of praying to a heated state" (Article 26, p. 133).

The Communist newspapers report with scorn that some Christians actually faint at their prayers. This is nothing new! St. John the Evangelist fainted when he saw the glorified Lord. It is too much for human nature. The Russian Christians have seen the glorified Lord again.

St. John was given the privilege of seeing his Lord because he had endured suffering for the cause of Christ. In his case—deportation to the island of Patmos. Today it is Christians in the Communist camp who are enduring suffering, and they have been accorded the honor of seeing the risen Christ who gives them comfort and light.

Sovetskaia Rossiia comments with scorn upon Christian women at prayer writhing in cramps on the floor, shouting and crying. It is not only Soviet newspapers that would view this with scorn. Respectable Western Christians would no doubt also consider this sort of prayer to be disgraceful. But I ask this question: did Jesus know how to pray? If the reply is that He didn't, then why should we pray in His name at all? If we conclude that Jesus did know how to pray, then we should note His manner. We read in Scripture that "in the days of His flesh ... He ... offered up prayers and supplications with strong crying and tears" (Heb. 5:7).

Of course, Western Christians also cry. They cry at their servants and waiters, and sometimes their wives and children. Many Western Christian ladies would shed a tear if a cup of a costly china service were to break. But weep over lost souls—that would be considered distasteful!

Although the documents presented in this book speak about oppression and suffering, we are not left with a gloomy impression. The Christians in Soviet Russia are joyful, confirming how right are those words of the poet Shelley:

> *"For when the power of imparting joy*
> *Is equal to the will, the human soul*
> *Requires no other end."*

The Christians jailed and tortured in Russia are spiritually in heaven. They have found the key to happiness which is the decision to serve Christ whatever the cost. Nor is their happiness a mere fool's paradise. Just as the astronomer in his observatory is overwhelmed with delight when he discovers a new galaxy, so these Christians have good cause for their joy. They have discovered a new reality. Their eyes have been opened and they are not afraid to speak of what they have seen. Before laughing Communist Courts they have daringly said: "I have seen Christ!"

Their testimony was the testimony of St. Paul and St. Joan and other holy people throughout the history of the Church. With them the words of Christ have found fulfillment: "Blessed are the pure in heart, for they shall see . . ." (Matt. 5:8).

And meanwhile—Section 227 of the Soviet Criminal Code states that men are not allowed to be zealous in prayer or to have visions! (*Sovietskaia Justitia*, May 1964). The Apostles could have been sentenced according to this law because they had seen the risen Lord and spoken with Him!

Human Soul Hunters

The God-ordained pastors of the Underground Church shine with exceptional beauty as they wear the dunces' caps accorded them by the Communists. I have shown how many of the phrases of scorn used in the Soviet Press are in fact the highest of commendations.

Take, for example, a phrase used in *Kazakhstanskaia Pravda*. That paper called some Christian pastors "human soul hunters" (Article 7, p. 73). What a beautiful name! Without knowing Our Lord's words about "fishers of man," the Communists echo this very theme. The newspaper poured scorn on one pastor, Korolink by name. It described that he "like a spider, spread his web to catch his next victim." What a compliment! *Pravda Vostoka* describes some preachers as "ardent" as if this were a wretched thing!

In the West I know of pastors who teach that "God is dead"; while others say that Jesus was a playboy or a homosexual. Some are destroyers of human souls, and some, like the priest and the Levite in the Parable of the Good Samaritan, simply do not care for souls. This is never true of a pastor in the Underground Church—he knows his true purpose in the world.

There is an old legend about the Lord. It tells how Jesus was once asked by one of His disciples about the meaning of the phrase in the book of Ecclesiastes "Vanity of vanities; all is vanity." Jesus—so the story goes—refused to answer the question, saying that the disciple was too young to understand. The young disciple soon forgot the whole matter.

Three years passed. Then one day Jesus said to the young disciple: "Come, let us take a walk together." The disciple was delighted at the suggestion and the two walked together for many miles.

It was a hot summer day in Palestine, and after a while Jesus said to the disciple: "I am tired. I will sit down here in the shadow of this tree. You are younger—go to the village that you can see near us, and bring me a jar of water." The disciple ran into the village, happy to be able to render his Master a service. He knocked at the first door he came to, hoping to get the jar of water, and it was opened by a girl who was unspeakably beautiful. When she opened her mouth to ask him what he wished, her voice was like the ringing of bells.

He could not tear himself away from the girl. They talked until evening and he found a place in the village to spend the night so that he could see her again the next morning. So it was for several days. He had fallen in love with her and she with him.

They married. She was of a rich family; so he received a large dowry. By hard work they made their estate even bigger. They had fields, vineyards, cattle, sheep and well-filled barns. She bore him three children.

Twelve years passed in fairy-tale happiness. Then disaster struck! A catastrophic flood swept away his house and all his belongings. His wife and three children drowned before his eyes. Only he escaped, but destitute and stripped of everything he had possessed. He wept over his lost happiness.

Suddenly he heard a voice from behind calling him. "Beloved disciple—did you bring me the jar of water as I asked?" The young man started up to find that he had been dreaming. He was deeply troubled.

"Master!" he said. "How could I forget your commandment?"

The Master's voice quietened him. "By your time twelve years have passed. By mine, only a quarter of an hour. I wanted to explain to you the meaning of the words 'Vanity of vanities; all is vanity!' "

Christians are spirits sent into the world to satisfy the Lord's thirst after saved souls. Christ has ordained from before the world's creation who should be the Ministers in His Church and most responsible for the salvation of souls. All is vanity compared to this most honorable of tasks.

We, in the West, often forget about it. So many minister to God only by the weekly sermon and perhaps a Bible Study. The ministers of the Underground Church are hunting souls every day—and the nights too! How high they are with God, and how mighty must they be in prayer!

In the Talmud it is said that a son of Rabban Yochanan became very ill. Yochanan turned to one of his disciples, Rabbi Chanina Ben Dosia, and said to him: "Chanina, my son, pray that my boy may live." Rabbi Chanina prayed and the son recovered. Then the wife of Rabban Yochanan asked him: "Is Chanina, your disciple, greater than you?"

Yochanan replied: "No, but he is like a servant before the king who has entry to him at any time, whereas I am like a minister who appears before the king only at fixed times and occasions."

Many ministers in the West do the work of God only on fixed times and occasions. Those behind the Iron Curtain don't know what rest is, and consequently their prayer life is continuous.

"Drunkards"

A frequent charge against pastors—such as the Hebrew Christian, Grunvald, from Alma Ata—is that of drunkenness (Article 15, p. 92). If there had been newspapers in the first century we would read of the same charge set against the apostles. Many Christians have been jailed in Rumania as drunkards, because they walked through the streets singing. Of course the charge is, in a sense, true! These men are drunk. Drunk with the Holy Spirit. Drunk with the joy of having the privilege to suffer. Like drunkards they sing in the street and in the trains.

Yes—and like drunkards they are always fighting! They take no account of the fact that they are like little Davids fighting mighty Goliaths.

The Communists think that they can ridicule the cause of Christ by saying that some of the pastors have an ugly past life. Sometimes these accusations may be true. They say of the Protestant pastor Drobkov, for example, that he had been a traitor to his fatherland in earlier times. Others are accused of having been thieves. From my side everything would be all right even if these accusations were true!

Jesus chooses His disciples from the "base things of the world, and things which are despised ... and things which are not, to bring to nought things that are" (I Cor. 1:28). The uglier the past history of these Christian pastors, the more beautiful their heroism appears as they take up the cross, face the dangers of the Underground Church, and go to prison for Christ who has washed them of their sins.

"Pentecostals"

The Pentecostals are a forbidden denomination in Russia. Because of this whenever the Soviet authorities arrest Christians of any kind, they often call them "Pentecostals."

Since 1948 no new religious congregation was allowed to register. No congregation is allowed to function unless it is registered with the Communist authorities. Therefore a vast number of churches are outlawed. These are what the Soviet Press often calls "Pentecostals," but the term is often misleading.

Further Charges

A study of the Communist Press reports shows us what charges are being brought against the Christians. One pastor is arraigned because he said: "God should take first place in our thoughts, feelings and deeds" (Article 7, p. 73). I cannot help comparing this with the session of the National Council of Churches in America held in Miami in 1967. There a poll of those who attended revealed that more than thirty per cent expressed doubt about the existence of a personal God. How much they could learn from the simple Christians who stand in the dock in Soviet Courts because of their dedication to the Creator!

Another charge is that these pastors have taught that the earthly life is merely a temporary existence, to be followed by the true life in heaven. Now the very aim of Communist philosophy is to crush such thinking. They want to convince caterpillars that they will never become multicolored butterflies able to flit from flower to flower! They want to convince buds that they will never burst into flowers! They cannot therefore tolerate a Christianity which teaches that the actual state of humanity is merely embryonic leading to the final development into a higher, angelic, Christlike being.

A frequent charge is that Christians opposed the forcible collectivization of agricultural property. In Rumania, Communists entered the villages and shot at random the first ten farmers they met. Then they asked the others to join the collective by signing a declaration stating that they were doing so of their own free will. With us it led to thousands of peasants being put in prison for refusing.

We read then of someone called Maerov saying: "I do not want to work together with the Antichrists" (Article 24, p. 122). For such words you have to suffer in the U.S.S.R.

Another courtroom charge against Christians is that their faith has brought about the destruction of families (Article 5, p. 60). This is not wholly untrue. Christ Himself said that He had not come to bring peace but division and that because of Him, daughters would be set against mothers, sons against fathers. This happens in the Communist camp.

With us conversion is dramatic. Let us imagine a young married couple who meet a Christian. The Christian witnesses for Christ. If the husband were to accept Christ as his Savior his wife would know that he stood a strong chance of being sent to prison. The Christian they had met would have been imprisoned and tortured several times before they had known him. She would face the prospect of weeping at the prison gate and raising her children in poverty. She had hoped for a happy home. This hope is gone if her husband becomes a Christian.

The wives and families of the Apostles must have faced this disruption of their family life. What must they have felt when they saw husbands, fathers and sons following a man who said that He personally would go to the cross, and would send His disciples into the world as sheep among wolves? So it is with us. Often the conversion of one member of the family produces violent reactions and even hatred from the other members. Sometimes the unconverted partner of a marriage will go to the Secret Police to denounce the one who wishes to "destroy" their happy family life. Sometimes wives commit suicide when the husband goes to baptism.

When I decided to be baptized, my wife was near to suicide. This was because we were Jews and among Jewish people there exists a great prejudice against baptism. So I was prepared somewhat for the Communist times in which such occurrences and the division of families have happened more frequently.

In Western churches we will read from time to time these words of Jesus: "If any man come to me, and hate not his father, and mother, and wife, and children, and brethren, and sisters, yea and his own life also, he cannot be my disciple" (Luke 14:26). In the Communist camp such words are becoming an everyday reality.

Dissenting family members are very often prosecution witnesses against their Christian relatives (Article 20, p. 107). What a tragedy it is when sons and daughters in Communist Courts put the dunces' caps on their parents— little knowing that they are thereby fulfilling a prediction of Christ.

But there are also other witnesses who stand in those courtrooms. Witnesses who, in the words of a Soviet newspaper, "raising their eyes toward the ceiling, invoke God, incomprehensibly mumbling something about conscience, about brothers and sisters in faith" (Article 7, p. 74).

The Christians who come to testify in the courtrooms of Russia do not merely represent themselves. They stand on the side of righteousness. The Communist newspapers may well dress them in the dunces' caps, mocking them as incomprehensible mumblers, but their beauty is not distorted by these unkind descriptions. They evoke God, they have consciences and they dare to proclaim themselves as brothers and sisters of those who go to prison for the faith.

Christians Lying

In the documents that follow we will see the Communist press accusing Christians on trial of prevaricating and trying to hide the truth (Article 25, p. 130). The word "Liar!" is written on the dunce's cap.

When David fled from Saul (I Sam. 21) he said to Ahimelech, the priest at Nob, that he was about the king's business. In a sense this was true. The King of Kings certainly had business involving David. He was to be the founder of a dynasty where the last heir would be Jesus, the eternal King. But Ahimelech would not have understood his words in this sense. Humanly speaking, then, David prevaricated.

We owe to the Communists, as to all men, the whole truth. But we are not obliged to reveal to all men all the facts about which they may inquire. Rather, we owe it to the Underground Church not to disclose its secrets to their persecutors. Our Christians have learned the truth in Christ's words concerning the need for combining the wisdom of serpents with the harmlessness of doves. They do not betray the activities of the Church before Communist judges or before examining officers.

Imprisonment

What is the attitude of Christians in the Communist camp to jail?

There is a story of Agesilaus, King of Sparta. When he was a child he was once put, by the director of some public games, in a place of very little importance. Others mocked him about this but he replied: "From my side it is all right. I will show that it is not the place that exalts the person, but it is the person that exalts and honors the place." The positions held by Stalin or Mao Tse-tung as dictators over hundreds of millions of people did not exalt them. Everyone knows that one has been a mass murderer and the other still is!

The Christians exalt and honor their prison cells. Where tyranny reigns, the prison cell becomes the most honorable of dwelling places. The prisons where Christians are detained become the camps of angels who surround and comfort them. There is nothing frightening in going to prison for Christ's sake.

Christian Divisions

The articles of the Soviet Press attack many types of Christians. They are as fierce against the Orthodox as they are against Baptists, Catholics, Pentecostals, Evangelicals, Seventh Day Adventists and others for whom Christianity is nothing else than sheer superstition and sometimes withcraft.

Communism hates Christianity in all its forms and this has made Christians of different variations feel as brethren to one another and join hands in fellowship. Under Communist pressure in prisons, Christians of widely different doctrines have become friends.

There is an old story of a Prince who lived in a city where elephants were unknown! One day he called all the blind men in the city together and put an elephant in their midst. Because there were so many of the blind men, no one could feel the whole animal. One could only feel the head, another the trunk, another the leg and so on. The blind men were later asked to describe the animal. The man who had touched the ear said that the elephant was a large pot. Another who had only touched the tail said that the animal was like a snake, and yet another who had touched the tusk said that it felt like a sword. Everyone described the animal according to the parts which he had touched.

With the things of God there is a similarity to the old tale. We see only in part—no one on earth knows the whole truth. In prison we discovered common ground: the faith in God, in Christ, in the Holy Spirit, in the scriptures and in eternal life.

So many deplore the divisions among Christians, but there exists no undivided religion because there exists no undivided humanity. No religion can be suited in the same form to the lowest grade of intelligence and also to the highest. We find among those brought before Communist Courts some with lofty spiritual experiences who remind us of Francis of Assisi and Thérèse of Lisieux. We find also some who have the most primitive notions about God and Christ. Christ is, with them, little more than a magical formula for healing diseases and getting out of trouble. Christianity has to be as diverse as humanity itself. But just as all men have their "humanity" in common, so Christians embracing diverse forms of worship suited to different types of culture and temperament have something in common. They share in the new humanity which is in Christ.

Doctrinal Purity

Sometimes I am asked if amidst this unity of Christians underground there are means of ensuring doctrinal purity. When such a question comes to me I can't help recalling the words of Shakespeare: "Tempest does not give leave to ponder."

Russia has practically no Bibles. In a country of 200 million inhabitants, the last 20,000 copies were printed in 1955—and this after a pause in printing of at least thirty years. Compare this figure against the figure of 3,666 registered baptisms in the Official Baptist Church for the one year of 1964. In addition, nobody can count the numbers of converts in the Underground Church or among the Orthodox and others. Records are not available. I repeat, Russia has practically no Bibles. A representative of the European Christian Mission asked a pastor if every Christian possessed at least a New Testament. (The *Anglican Digest,* organ of the Episcopal church of U.S.A., estimates in its January 1968 issue that forty-five million Russians practice their religion "underground." Where are the Bibles for all these?) The answer he was given was that he should rather be asking if every *church* owned a New Testament. And if there are practically no Bibles, how much less can we expect there to be textbooks on Christian doctrine, or theological magazines.

There are, apparently, two religious quarterlies published in Moscow. One is Orthodox, the other is Baptist. I showed a copy of the Baptist magazine to a Russian Baptist physician who happened at our time of meeting to be outside Russia. He told me he had never seen it before. There is a Rumanian newspaper full of patriotic and religious articles called *The Voice of the Fatherland,* but I never saw it on sale in Rumania! These magazines have it as their main purpose to dupe Westerners.

Who is right to demand doctrinal purity from Christians who have never seen a book of doctrine? By chance of birth or circumstances of conversion they know their religion by different names—"Catholicism," "Orthodoxism," "Pentecostalism." Basically, their religion is love toward God and neighbor, and faith in Christ. To those Christians many of the doctrinal controversies of the Western Churches seem very strange.

We have a story. Two farmers were friends. One evening they sat together on a bench and looked at the starry sky. One of them said: "I would like to have pastureland as big as the area of the sky we see!"

The other said: "I would rather have as many sheep as there are stars up there!"

"But if you had so many sheep," said the first, "where would you graze them all?"

"On your pasture," replied the first. "It's big enough!"

The first began to cry: "How dare you come with your sheep onto my pasture!"

The one had no pasture, the other had no sheep, and they quarreled over things they didn't possess! I believe that we Christians, also, are continually quarreling over things that we often really don't know.

How many theologians ever stop to realize how much geography affects doctrinal discussions? How does one explain to a Christian in the Lubi tribe in Upper Volta or to a brother among the Auca Indians of Ecuador or to a believer of a tribe in the Bering Strait area (where they have a language consisting of sixty words), the difference between pre-Millennialism and post-Millennialism? I do not mean to imply by this that doctrinal thought and teaching is unimportant. Far from it. What I want to stress is the difference between faith in Christ and the various theoretical expressions of that faith which we call theological doctrines.

I hope that the cultivated and advanced Western Christians will accept our primitive faith as genuine. Wherever "two or three are gathered together" in the name of Christ, the Savior is there also. The aim of these simple Soviet Christians is the glory of God. If they were to come to the West they would probably become as puzzled people as I am myself! How would they know how to choose from innumerable Churches that all claim to be Biblical and to be more in the right than the others?

Whether we like it or not, the simple fact is that the Underground Church in Russia is very little concerned about doctrinal matters. It is difficult to see how it could be otherwise. There are, perhaps, theologians in the West who will be shocked by this. They would hold that salvation depends upon a grasp of true doctrine. I can only plead that they do not, in fact, have the great reformers on their side.

Bishop Latimer, during his trial by the Catholics, was asked if he considered all his Catholic predecessors were damned because they believed in such things as holy images and prayers to the Virgin Mary, a faith which he did not share. His answer was as follows: "God knows his elect and diligently watches and keeps them, so that all things serve to their salvation. The nature of fire is to burn all that is laid in it. Yet God kept the three young men in Babylon, that they burnt not. . . . So false doctrine burns as the fire; it corrupts. But God kept his elect, that they were not corrupted with it, but always put their trust in the one everliving God, through the death of Jesus Christ our Lord. In Elias' time, idolatry and superstition reigned, so that Elias said: 'Lord, they have destroyed Thy altars and slain Thy prophets and preachers, and I am left alone.' But the Lord answered him: 'I have reserved to myself seven thousand men, who have not bowed their knees to Baal.' So God, I trust, reserved our forefathers, in so perilous times, more graciously than we think."

This answer of Latimer's made clear that it was possible to belong to a Church considered by some Protestants as idolatrous and erroneous, and still be saved. Enlightened Catholics think the same about Protestants.

Instead of demanding doctrinal purity, it would be more positive to unite with the Underground Church against the official leaders of the Russian Churches who are, in fact, merely stooges of the Communists. Centuries ago when Caecilian was elected Bishop of Carthage in the year 311, a party rose up against him objecting that his ordination was not valid. This was because he had been ordained by Felix, Bishop of Artunga, who had been a traitor during times of persecution, delivering up the Scriptures to the heathen magistrates to be burnt. But men who have done far worse than Felix conduct ordinations now in the Baptist and Orthodox churches. They have given up their brethren to death. They are the ones about whom it is said in the Bible: "They crucify to themselves the Son of God afresh, and put Him to an open shame" (Heb. 6:6).

The Documents

You will find in the documents that follow dramas and victories. You will meet children who have dared to ruin their future careers and even endanger their own lives and the lives of their parents. They have said to their school-teachers: "You, teachers, lie to us. Everything on earth has been created by God."

Now we will leave the documents to speak for themselves. We have not presented all the documents that could have been set out. We could have shown how bulldozers have flattened churches in Tashkent, Brest and Vladivostok. We could have shown Christians being sacked because of their faith. We could have shown expulsions from University, confiscation of property, Christians put in asylums and many other things, as disturbing of church services by volleyball matches in the churchyard, organized on Sunday mornings by the Communist youth. (This explains the case of priest Turkovskii, p. 56). May these documents suffice! May they awaken the Christians of the free world to what is happening to their brothers in Communist countries now, and to what could happen to themselves in the future.

1961

Source: *Uchitelskaia Gazeta* (Teacher's Gazette), June 18, 1961

1

Whose Fate is the Director's Concern?

From the Courtroom:

The judges enter!

The talking stops, those present stand up. The traditional phrase imposes an inner composure upon the people. I can see how their faces become stern, especially the faces of those two who sit, apart from the rest, alone, by the window. Rows of empty chairs, like a fence, separate them from the audience, a wide aisle—from the judges' bench. Two—in an emptiness.

His red beard is broad and thick, his hair pulled back, his eyes cast down; this is how Ignatii Semenovich Mullin looks. Spiritual humbleness does not match at all with his heavyset body, sparkling with health. On the other hand, Maria Iakovlevna is the complete opposite of her husband: a little downtrodden woman, continuously crying in the corner of a handkerchief, hardly reaching his shoulders. He is the head of the family—a "godgiven" one. He gives orders. Now the simple term "respondent" receives a special meaning. Citizen Mullin is held to respond for the reasons why his daughter, Evdokiia, left home.

They say, there is no other girl in the fifth grade more industrious and studious than Dusia (diminutive of Evdokiia). During the teaching period she would not speak a word; during the recess, you could not make her come out to the hall—she would sit at her desk, read and prepare her lessons. Her collar is the whitest, her uniform the best pressed. Indeed, such children are not often found in school.

In a small town there are few big secrets. And, although Mullin's house is closed to strangers, the children revealed: they are *Staroveri* [Old-believers]. This news reached the class supervisor, Mrs. Maria Konstantinovna Aldarkina.

Well, this explains this attentiveness in school (they would not let her study at home), the books read during

47

recess (the parents do not allow reading), the uniform so white and starched (an example for the "worldly" ones). Even during the school hours Dusia was not allowed to forget about God.

What does she say about her home? The day starts and ends with prayers. Three daughters (the youngest is four years of age) fervently pray and make deep bows. In turn, when relatives gather together in the evening, the father praises the daughters without end. Hearing him, the childless aunt makes a sign of the cross, smiles benevolently and nods: "When I die, I'll leave everything to you, Ignat."

Behind the quiet, one-syllable answers of Dusia, the teacher sensed a tragedy. The little girl felt her situation as a burden. It was obviously difficult for her to lead this double life, to be torn between the school and the house, to pray and (at the same time) read interesting books. Thus, Maria Konstantinovna picked the only right way, though it might have looked, at first sight, a roundabout one. She did not try, right away, to convince Dusia that there was no God. After all, at the age of ten, a person could not be regarded as believing. Rather, it was a habit, still without realization, which does not fit at all the entire way of life of a pupil. Maria Konstantinovna decided that it was this way of life that should win the case.

Gradually and consistently, Dusia became used to behaving in school the same way as her classmates. She participated in the editing of the wall newspaper and read poems at evening gatherings.

"Do you pray?" Maria Konstantinovna inquired.

"Yes, I do," Dusia replied.

"Do you believe?"

"No, but I am scared of the parents . . ."

Perhaps she was afraid, perhaps she did not want to complain.

Presently, Dusia acquired new, good and useful habits and duties and it was necessary to talk about them openly. At one of the parents' meetings, it was in the sixth grade, Aldarkina started a conversation with Dusia's mother. As soon as Maria Konstantinovna mentioned that "she should be allowed to join the Pioneers (Communist children's organization) and to read at home," Mullina pursed her lips:

"Our religion forbids it. We are—'Old-believers.' It is a sin to read, it is a sin to wear a scarf. Everything is a sin."

Next day, Dusia came to school sad and quiet.

"It would be better, Maria Konstantinovna, if you would not talk," she said during the recess.

"What happened, did they scold you?"

"They did."

"Did they beat you?"

"They did, too. . . ."

This was an open declaration of war, but Dusia decided not to surrender. She became more stern and quiet. Everything indicated that a fight was going on at home.

"Perhaps I should visit your home," Maria Konstantinovna once asked.

"No," Dusia replied.

But soon it was necessary to make that visit. This happened during the last week of Lent, after the hungry and weakened Dusia had been fed by her schoolmates. They went together with the teacher of history, Shapovalenko.

They were not admitted beyond the kitchen. Mrs. Mullin stood up, barred the door and stood there during the entire conversation.

The conversation was not much different from that previously held in school. The mother, on the one hand, complained that Dusia helped at home too little; she sweeps the floor only twice a week; on the other hand, she repeated again: "It is a sin—to read."

The mentioning of the fast made her mad:

"We fasted and will continue to fast. I can do without meat. . . ."

With this, they left. And the next day, Dusia declared in school that she wouldn't go home any more. Why? The best answer is contained in her letter to the editor mailed by her teacher, Aldarkina:

"I left home. I left it for ever. I am forbidden to be a Pioneer, I am not allowed to read fine literature, I am not allowed to make friends with my schoolmates, to do community work, to attend evening events in school, movies, theaters; they say nasty things about our school. I am not going home."

For a few days, Dusia stayed with her friends. Then she was placed in a boarding school. There, a line of aunts, headed by her mother, came to see her. "Come home," they whispered into Dusia's ear. "Whatever has happened,

you have your family, your sisters. You should always
think of them."

So, Dusia went home for the May 1st holiday. Even the
Court was not able to establish what happened at home.
Yet, upon her return to the boarding school, the girl firmly
declared: "I am not going there any more!"

Only now it has become clear that it was not their child
the Mullins were concerned about. They were worried
about their own reputation in the eyes of their own relatives
and fellow believers. They were concerned about the in-
heritance which the rich aunt had promised her godchild. It
was their intention to use all kinds of tricks to lure Dusia
home and then quickly move to another town, mix with
strange people and forget the unpleasant incident.

No, it was impossible to leave the child in such a family.
This is why the school and the community of parents filed
a petition to deprive the Mullins of their parental power.

Dusia asked the Soviet people for help and received it.
Our Constitution allows everybody to believe in God, but
the Law forbids forcing religious ideas even upon children.

"Say, Mullin," the judge asks, "if your daughter returns
home, will you continue to make her pray?"

"Well, what harm will it do for her if she crosses her
forehead?"

*"Does it mean that, in choosing between God and your
daughter, you choose God?"*

"I will not abandon my faith"—the man said gloomily.

The Court deprived the Mullins of their parental powers
and obligated them to pay the costs of the boarding school
for their daughter.

In a detailed substantiation of the verdict, directed to the
school, the inadequate atheistic work among children was
pointed out.

.   .   .

I hardly returned to Moscow from my assignment when
a letter came to the editor. And here is what it said: "The
day after the trial, there assembled in the school its director
Zakirov, *partorg* [party organizer] Kashapov and *zavuch*
[principal of the teaching staff] Mrs. Andreevshaia. The
teacher, Mrs. Aldarkina, was summoned. It is difficult
briefly and clearly to reproduce the conversation of the
four people, which lasted two hours with three people

against one. Apparently, teacher Aldarkina had deceived
the entire staff and destroyed all the good things that the
school had achieved due to the leadership of the director
[it was alleged]: Aldarkina did not work with the Mullins!
Why didn't she reeducate them in order to avoid the break
in the family? Now, the management of the school was to
take the blame. . . . Aldarkina brought about the trouble
upon their heads by contacting the newspaper. As if, without the interference of the editors, the matter would not
have become known. . . ."

I am trying to find out how well Zakirov and Kashapov
"investigated" the fate of Dusia Mullin.

"When did it become known to you that the Mullins
oppressed their daughter?" I asked the director.

"After the girl left home."

"Are there other believers in the school?"

"I don't know. There are several hundreds of pupils in
the school. You cannot watch all of them. . . ."

Many people got involved in Dusia's fate: the Chief of
the Region, Sadreev, the principal of the boarding school,
Popova, employees of the Court and of the Prosecutor's
office—all of them had Dusia in mind. But the director had
just himself in mind in the first place. When the girl left
home, he called the parents into his office and, in a long
discussion, tried to convince Mullin to give his promise
that he would *stop persecuting his daughter*. And, although
it was known from Dusia, her friends and neighbors that
such a "promise" would not carry any weight, Zakirov
continued to insist upon having it. Apparently, in such
case, Dusia could be sent back home, left with her family
and, naturally, peace would come to the school. Then,
nobody would dare to blame the director for the *lack of
educational and antireligious work*. It was only Mullin's
fanaticism that upset his attempts to "settle" the matter out
of Court.

Actually, the trial itself did not particularly upset Zakirov. From the moment she went to the boarding school, she
ceased to be regarded as a pupil of his school. This is why
the director did not go to see her and talk to her. He only
attended the final session of the Court.

It was that special reference to his school that upset him
most. And it was the reason for the dispersal (*sic*). Zakirov
and Kashapov understand the honor of the teaching staff in
a peculiar way. They confuse honor with personal, private

tranquility and this is their only concern. Well, *now there is plenty of reason for them to be concerned.*

Town of Bugulma,
Tatar Autonomous S.S.R.

L. Strizhovskii,
Special correspondent

1962

Source: *Komsomolskala Pravda,* June 21, 1962

2

A Sect of Fanatics Was Exposed

From the Courtroom:

Kharkov, June 20th. (T.A.S.S.) The assizes of the District Court of Kharkov tried *the criminal case against the accused leaders of, and active participants in, the religious sect of* Piatidesiatniki (*Pentecostals*) *which existed illegally in Kharkov.*

There were in the dock—*the leader of the sect N. M. Kozelko who, just a few years ago, returned from prison where he served his term for a serious crime,* preachers G. V. Zinchenko, N. T. Rubashka, I. P. Garkavii, F. M. Chubenko and M. T. Durtan.

During the preliminary investigation and during the trial it was established that the activities of this religious sect harmed the health of the citizens and was combined with infringement of their civil rights and with forcing them to refuse to fulfill their social obligations.

It became known at the trial that, for example, I. Zinchenko, A. Rubleva, A. Pavlenko and S. Rzhevskaia became victims of the sectarians.

Witnesses—teachers of school No. 39 in Kharkov, which the children of the accused Rubashka attend, gave the Court a picture of the detrimental influence of the sectarians on the children. *The parents taught their children to keep away from everything worldly,* from our outstanding work, and *prepared the youngsters for the so-called "life after death."*

The Court completely unmasked the hypocrites. Under the impact of evidence, even the most ardent leaders of the sect were forced to admit that they were tried justly.

The Court passed a decision under which *N. M. Kozelko was sentenced to five years in prison with confiscation of his property and deportation, after serving the sentence, to faraway places of the Soviet Union for another five years.* N. T. Rubashka and I. P. Garkavii were sentenced to three years in prison each, G. V. Zinchenko and M. T. Durtan—

to one and a half years in prison each. F M. Chubenko, who admitted the harmfulness of his activities as a preacher and declared that he would leave the sect, was sentenced to conditional punishment with a probation term of three years, and was released from custody.

Source: *Izvestiia,* June 28, 1962

3

The Shyness of Power

The following event happened at the village of Novoiurevskoe, in the Tambov Region. A big, husky young man approached a little boy, seized him by his collar and tossed him several meters away. The teacher, indignant, approached.

The hooligan replied:

"Your puppy was in my way."

The teacher went to see the Chief of the regional unit of Militsia, N. Rozhnov.

"Catch the hooligan!"

"Right away, we'll teach him a lesson," the chief of militia sternly replied. "Who was it, did you say, that harmed the boy? Oh, Turkovskii. Well ... the matter is complicated..."

Girls and boys played volleyball. Suddenly the same husky youth appeared on the court.

"Stop the game. Find yourselves another place."

"But the court has always been here. We do not disturb anybody."

"Is that so? You don't want to do it voluntarily?" With a metallic voice the youth said and shouted: "Hey, Orthodox, come and liquidate the court!"

At this instant, a few men came running, dug out the posts, tore down the net; the children sadly went to complain to the Prosecutor.

N. Bokarev, in charge of the Regional Prosecutor's office, was also indignant.

"This is, you know not a minor act of hooliganism. This should be punished by jail.... Just tell me about him. What is his name?"

"Turkovskii," the children replied.

"Turkovskii?" The Prosecutor cooled off immediately. "This is another story...."

Some time afterwards Turkovskii stripped a band from the sleeve of a *druzhinnik* [volunteer civilian policeman], Viktor Likhachev, and tore his jacket.

"Why didn't you bring the hooligan to his senses? No guts?" we inquired.

"Well, I could have ... But it's forbidden.·... I myself could be jailed. Why? After all, Comrade Iartsev himself knows about that hooligan, but he does not take any action against him...."

True enough, the Chairman of the Regional Executive Committee of Staroiurevskoe, V. Iartsev, is well informed about everything. But he, too, when hearing the name of Turkovskii, becomes uneasy:

"You see ..."

The whole secret proves to lie in the fact that Turkovskii is the local minister. This fact worries the local leaders quite a bit. If it were a normal Soviet citizen, a tractor driver, a locksmith, a physician or agronomist, that had committed the excesses, he would be brought to his senses immediately. But how to deal with a violent minister?

We talked to many leaders of the Soviet (council) of Novoiurevskoe and of the Staroiurevskoe Region, with *druzhinniki*, propagandists and workers on the cultural front. And we had strange conversations.

They were strange because literally none of them were concerned with the question of how to oppose the influence of the churchmen and sectarians, but rather to secure their tranquility. Obviously, our partners in conversation can send in a correction of this statement: "We never said anything like this." Well, then if so, how should we evaluate the case of the volleyball court? This court is located not far from the church but not on its territory. Yet, instead of curbing the aggressive minister, they endlessly discuss in the region the question: was the volleyball court built far enough from, or too close by the church.

We do not stretch the point. The village House of

Culture is also near the church. And the minister forbade playing the radio and records in the club. The school is not far away. The minister categorically demands that no physical exercises be conducted in the fresh air outside of the school (because this would also be in front of the church). Furthermore, one of the points of Turkovskii's ultimatum is to stop antireligious propaganda in the village.

In our talks, we repeatedly hear the escape thesis: naturally, we have sufficient power, but wouldn't we hurt the feelings of those believing?

May we be permitted to ask: since when have the volleyball game, the dance music or physical exercise become offensive to the believing people? (If somebody feels offended, it is his private matter.)

Can a Pioneer be beaten for urging his friend not to go to church? Who gave the permission to attack the *druzhinnik* who is performing his duties? In short, we intend to put the question like this: what about the feeling of nonbelievers, can they be offended?

Prosecutor Comrade Bokarev basically agrees with all our statements.

"But we still should not touch the minister. The unpleasantness that might follow would be too much. . . ."

"What kind?" The Prosecutor makes a gesture of undetermined meaning. "Why do you ask me? The Regional Committee and the Regional Executive Committee know about it, too. . . ."

"There is no doubt about it that Turkovskii will be tried," the Chairman of the Regional Executive Committee assures us.

But this is not all that the inhabitants of the village of Novoiurevskoe need.

"Naturally, the hooligan should be tried according to his merits," they say. "But why should we exchange one useless thing for another? *We do not want to get just a 'good' minister. What we need is that the church be closed, because it became a spreader of scandals and active religious propaganda outside of its wall.*"

This is the demand of those five thousand inhabitants of the village of Novoiurevskoe. As we can see, this demand is not without substantiation. But it proved to be impossible to carry it out. *A church may be closed only at the request of the believers themselves, and, naturally, no believer would request it.*

We understand very well that this matter cannot be dealt with by shooting from the hip. Naturally, there is a great majority of nonbelievers at any settlement. But it would not be right to settle such delicate matters mechanically, by simple voting. We respect the freedom of conscience of every citizen and we are not entitled to forbid them to perform their religious practices.

However, the church of Novoiurevskoe has turned from a place where these religious rites are performed into an active propaganda center of ignorance, and into a direct violator of Soviet laws. Why then, as the people of Novoiurevskoe demand, could not this church which openly violates our laws be closed? Yes, close the church, don't just change the pastor! This would be a just settlement.

After all, the core of the matter lies not in this particular church and its servant. The local Association for the spreading of political and scientific knowledge showed us an extensive program of scientific-atheistic lectures: in the regional department of cultural affairs they told us about antireligious evening programs, exhibits, etc. All this is fine. But these lectures and programs are arranged for convinced atheists. As a rule, they have an instructive character. *And it is not an accident that the number of sectarians does not diminish in the region; rather often young couples are married in church, and a young mother takes her baby to church to be baptized. . . .*

We were told: "Well, you are talking about a militant, offensive antireligious propaganda. But how can it be done? The believers cannot be dragged by force into the clubs."

But, for example, could not an "attack" be made by a massive exposure of the way of life of the pastor of Novoiurevskoe, or of the scandals coming from the walls of the church? Is it not permissible to talk about all this quite aloud at the village meetings? It can be done. And then this will be heard by the participating believers and those hesitating. But now, if we should be frank, even people far from being religious bitterly smile:

"Whatever Father Nikolai wants, he will do. That's power."

You must admit that such statements do not help the success of atheistic propaganda.

Not long ago, *some fanatics—sectarians of Staroiurevskoe—were deprived of parental powers. Should not such events become a topic for widespread talks not only about the essence of the religious belief but also about its humanity and cruelty?* Yes, if everything is told, the hearts of many believers might shudder. Well, the local atheists did not use these opportunities.

We have a powerful weapon in our fight against religious influence, and ignorance. On our side is the truth, the truth about the universe and about the laws which govern it. But I think that the enlightenment alone might not be enough. If the sectarians inflict an injury to the souls of children, and, sometimes, to their bodies, if they drive people to psychiatric hospitals—they should be punished with all severity of the law. If the minister commits excesses and the church becomes a breeding ground for lawbreaking and for active religious propaganda and lawlessness, we are not only entitled but obligated to take the most determined measures. Soviet laws also apply to a citizen in clerical garb.

Village of Novoiurevskoe,
Tambov Region

V. Komov, Iu. Feofanov,
Special correspondents of *Izvestiia*

Source: *Kazakhstanskaia Pravda* (Kasakstan Truth), January 7, 1962.

4

Under the Domination of Obscurity

Early in the morning the inhabitants of the city of Ush Tobe were awakened by earsplitting cries. People hurried to the house No. 60 on Vodoprovodna Street. They carried out of the house three men poisoned to death by the fumes of carbon monoxide. Two of them were brothers, Petr and Iakov Kirichko.

The mother of the dead—a sectarian—was tearing her hair, wringing her hands and shedding tears.

"Why, dear God? Why, for what sins do You punish me? Please make my sons alive again, be merciful!"

The reason for the tragedy was the fact that one of the brothers—Iakov—quarreled with his brother Petr and the latter's friend P. Sirota, while attempting to make them join the sect. When he saw that his attempts failed, he closed, for the night, the chimney of the stove with the fire burning inside.

Baptists is the name of the members of one of the most reactionary religious sects. They attempt to catch in their nets as many victims as possible, to confuse people's minds and *to undermine their will power.* The leaders of the sect teach their flock: do not attend movies or theaters; do not engage in sports; *do not sing, except pious songs;* do not read fine literature!

The leaders of the Baptist sect pay special attention to people who find themselves in a difficult situation or a plight, and to inexperienced boys and girls.

We do not have to look far for an example. Here is one Nadezhda Nikolenko—a young person of undetermined occupation or place of abode. Her task is—to recruit "souls" to the sect. It was *she* who, *pretending to be a nurse, visited a young* Komsomol [*Communist Youth Association*] *member in his home. She tried to get him to join the sect.* Yet, this time the sectarian was clearly mistaken. When she realized that she would be exposed, she disappeared.

And here is another striking event which shocked the whole community of Ush Tobe. The religious fanatics Anatolii and Gennadii Pogodzev bestially beat up their own brother, Valerii, a worker at the Karatalskii *Mezhkolkhostroi* [intercollective farm management].

It is Sunday. . . . Everybody tries to use his day reasonably; attending movies, visiting a library and the stadium, relaxing with his family. . . . But what is it over there? *Some people, looking around like thieves, are sneaking along Kirov Street toward house No. 44.*

We saw a disgusting scene when we entered that house. Over twenty praying people, kneeling and raising their arms, uttered earsplitting sounds, tore their hair and, in a wild orgy, hit the floor with their heads. *Here, along with adults, were also children.* Terrified, tormented, they stood there crowded in a corner, and cried. One of them was Zoia Iusupova. She was only six years old.

We talked to one of the chief preachers of the Baptist sect, Ivan Grechikhin.

"We bring up our children," he said, *"in fear of God. Therefore, three times a week, we conduct prayer sessions."*

It cannot be said that people of the town do not know about all this. But the Karatalskii Regional Party Committee decided that it was a "family" affair in which one should not interfere.

Meeting no opposition on the part of the Communists or the community, the sectarians at Ush Tobe let themselves go.

The Subbotniki *(Adventists),* Piatidesiatniki, *the Evangelists and others recruit to their sects not only adults, but even children of preschool age.*

In the city of Ush Tobe, fifty "houses of agitators" were established, which were expected to become centers of individual work with the believers, to arrange Sunday readings and evenings of questions and answers. But, having established them (the houses) the workers of the regional Party Committee forgot all about the needed control and checkup of the work of the propagandists and agitators, and neglected this important sector of the ideological activity.

In the Karatalsk Region, there is a division of the Society for the Promotion of Political and Scientific Knowledge. The members of the Society read twenty lectures on atheistic topics. But all of them were read to atheists. True, once they tried to assemble the believers, but the talks with them were carried out to such an extent unconvincingly and incompetently that many of those gathered did not even know why they were summoned.

The activists do not approach the citizens with clear and fervent talks. Some Communists do not even give a good example of bringing up their own families. *The father of the Communist Petr Grechikhin, the secretary of the* Komsomol, *the Center of Technical Inspection of the Ush Tobe station, is the head of the Baptist community; Petr's wife is also a sectarian.* It is obvious that P. Grechikhin shows lack of principles, bargaining with his conscience and yielding to ignorance and obscurantism.

Our Soviet reality, our ideas and our scientific achievements disperse the darkness of superstitions. Believing people in ever-growing numbers free themselves from the religious chain; many preachers abandon their sects. But our Party teaches us that, in the field of antireligious propaganda, we should not rely on leaving things to themselves. It is necessary, thoughtfully and persistently, to explain to the believers the evil of religious superstitions, and to conduct an active atheistic propaganda.

A struggle against the manifestations of the bourgeois ideology and morality, superstitions and prejudices, constitutes a component part of the work in the field of Communist education of the workers.

"It is necessary," the Program of the Communist Party of the Soviet Union states, "systematically to conduct a widespread scientific-atheistic propaganda, patiently to explain the inconsistencies of religious beliefs which came to being in the past on the basis of the domination of the elemental forces of nature over the people, and social oppression due to the ignorance of the essential causes of natural and social phenomena."

Unfortunately, the Party organizations of the Karatalskii Region do not yet work adequately on the fulfillment of this task, as stated by the Program of the Communist Party of the Soviet Union. In the scientific-atheistic propaganda work, too many technicalitics are admitted, too little individual work is conducted with the believers. This is the reason why, at Ush Tobe, many people still walk blindly in the darkness of superstitions.

Ush Tobe,
Region of Alma Ata

N. Shakhov,
Our special correspondent

Source: *Komsomolskaia Pravda*, July 5, 1962

5

The "Quakers" Tremble with Fear from Responsibility

From the Courtroom:

There are four of them sitting with gloomy faces in the dock. Four leaders of the *Piatidesiatniki*—Pentecostals, *one of the most* reactionary and *fanatic* sects. They lived in Krasnodon. During the occupation, suddenly and openly Chernetskii would walk its streets in a Hitlerite uniform, Yes, it was the same streets on which young Guardsmen secretly pasted posters and moved to their assignments.

The past of the others—Mazhnikov, Kolesnichenko and Kazimirov—was not much better. Having served lenient punishments, they still had the chance to enter on the proper pathway. Instead, those grabbers and obscurantists organized stinking subversion. Now, in the free and happy city of Krasnodon, they were forced to hide from the world. *The "brothers and sisters in Christ" met during dark nights. Exhausting prayer practices* started which turned to frenzy, trembling and hysterics. All this was needed by the scum in order to terrify their "brothers and sisters" and make them blindly submit to their will.

The electro-inspector, Sofia Trofimovna Breeva, told the Court about the shocking family tragedy.

"We had a nice family. My daughter was growing. My husband, *Nikolai Bielitskii, worked as a machinist and was in good repute. But he became a* Piatidesiatnik. *He started attending prayer meetings and spent his days and nights there*. When his fellow workers learned about it and started suggesting that he break with the sectarians, he decided to submit a letter of resignation [to his factory]. At that time, I was sick and bedridden in the hospital with our daughter. Yet my husband refused to help me during my hard time. This is the value of their "love thy neighbor" [belief]. For a year and a half Nikolai would not work, having turned into a lazy do-nothing who lived off the charity of the sectarians. One day I decided to watch my husband in his "zeal."

Before my eyes, a healthy man whom I loved, turned into a spineless creature, a madman. *Tears ran down his face* and lather appeared upon his mouth. Up to now, I tremble from aversion. No, it was impossible to love such a person. After long quarrels and persuasions we parted. Please punish with all the severity of the Soviet Laws *those who broke up our happiness and our family.*"

The sect has also other victims charged to its account. Their entire activity had a direct antisocial character. The Pentecostals in pretty Krasnodon hate everything: the factories, schools, libraries and movies.

"I was dragged into the sect," nineteen-year-old Zotkina testified, "but I soon realized where the *Piatidesiatniki* were pulling me. My friends who opened my eyes helped me. I thank them. I started hating prayers and the people who wanted to bury me alive."

But perhaps most striking was the appearance at the trial of the mother of a murdered young Guardsman, Polina Dmitrievna Lopukhova, a teacher at the Gorkii school. For some time she has been waging a courageous war for the son of the sectarians, Sasha Plotnikov.

"We are not going to allow the fanatics to destroy the lives of our children," Polina Dmitrievna said in conclusion.

For three days, the People's Court of the Krasnodon Region deliberated in the "Young Guard" Cultural Center. For three days hundreds of people witnessed the exposure of the criminal activities of *Piatidesiatniki*. The fanatics got their just rewards for depriving Soviet people of the joy of creative work, for hurting their human dignity, for jeering the weak and cheated ones and robbing them (no wonder that the "Brother preachers" had good private residences and motorcycles).

The Court sentenced the leaders of the sect of *Piatidesiatniki*, Kolesnichenko and Kazimirov, to five years in prison with subsequent deportation for the same period of time; Chernetskii and Mahnikov were also given prison terms.

Lugansk
L. Alekseeva
Is. Svintitskii

Source: *Ogoniok* (Little Flame), March 13, 1962

6

Behind Closed Shutters

"Well, Iasha, recite your assignment," the "lady teacher" says.

"*. . . I look for the resurrection of the dead,*" the slim boy, nine years old, says quickly.

"Good boy. . . . And now, do explain when all this is going to happen."

Fear appears in the boy's blue eyes. Can it really happen that his grandmother might return from the grave and again get hold of his ear with her bony fingers?

"*The resurrection of the dead will come,*" the "teacher" softly suggests, "*during the second advent of Christ. And now, children, let's repeat it all together.*"

Three dozen voices join in reciting.

On the outside, behind the walls of *this house in which the teaching of God's laws is conducted*, a normal life is carried on on this Sunday.

Young people crowd by the newspaper stand selling *Komsomolets Kubani*. In the movie theater "Oktabrj" [October], filled to capacity, the picture *First Flight to the Stars* is shown. The huge Hall of the Pioneers has been since early in the morning occupied by the young tillers of the soil.

But neither the regional nor the provincial committees of popular education, whose task it is to know, direct and head popular education, knows about the existence of the above-mentioned "school" in the very center of the Krasnodar Province, in the very City of Krasnodar.

Strange things happen to the pupils of the Sunday School, who, during the rest of the week, are pupils of regular public schools.

For example, in the school No. 41, in the second grade "C," a lesson of singing is under way.

"Little eagle, little eagle, fly above the Sun," all students sing in a ringing voice. Only the slim boy of nine does not sing. He sits there, with his head down, sadly covering his mouth with his little hand.

"Forbidden, forbidden," answers Iasha Stepaniuga, to all attempts of the teacher to make him sing, and he cries bitterly.

Iasha's sister, Liuda, is the only girl in grade six who did not join the Pioneers.

In school No. 23, there is a girl, twelve years old, Vali Andreeva. Recently she took off her Pioneer scarf: "I believe in God and God does not approve."

Viktor Bogomaz is finishing the tenth grade. Although he does not mind drawing some visual-aid articles for the school, *he regards the Bible as the most important visual-aid of them all. . . .*

In school No. 39 . . . This sad list could be continued. We were correct counting about thirty pupils of the "Sunday School." But, even if, from the windows of the Committee on popular education they cannot see every single pupil, in school, pupils of the type of Iasha Stepaniuga cannot be overlooked. And yet, here is what the senior girl Pioneer leader of the school No. 23, Tamara Karpenko, excitedly tells me about how actively her Pioneers work. On the card of her region, there are all kinds of conventional markings: an axe, a book, a doll. . . . In the house marked by an axe, wood needed to be chopped, as the inhabitant is an invalid; books are read to old people; the little girl whom her mother leaves alone will be comforted with dolls. All these are good deeds. But neither Tamara Karpenko nor the head teacher, Postnov, nor the lecturer, Mrs. Lugovaia, who *finished special courses for antireligious work*, can tell me in what way they pull out their pupils from the religious quagmire. . . .

On the other hand, the sectarians—well, they work actively and firmly stick to "their" pupils. Naturally, it is not easy to make people study biblical legends at the time when Gargarin orbits in the space. Not everybody is ready to bite even the bait in the form of free soup generously offered at the prayer meetings. First to fall in are usually the children of the sectarians, who yield to the will of the parents. It is terrifying to think in whose dirty paws is the fate of such "pupils": the "School" was set up on the initiative of the hardened sectarians Dubovchenko and Kirillov, who were sentenced in the past for anti-Soviet activities, and of one Kobzar, who served his term for robbery.

What is the future of Iasha Stepaniuga? Will he become the same as Eudokiia Brydnia, the same "teacher" who teaches prayers to children in the Sunday School? . . .

When they found out at the worsted cloth factory about the dark deeds of Eudokiia, the workers got angry. Brydnia was told to discontinue her infamous occupation.

"For the present, I'll discontinue," she agreed gloomily, *"but in the future, I'll do what my conscience tells me to."*

This conscience, directed by the experienced hand of such people as Dubovchenko and Kobzar, suggested to her other forms of sectarian propaganda: to visit homes and fill childish heads with religious rubbish.

When I asked, at the combine factory, in what brigade (group) Eudokiia Brydnia was working, I was told first one, then another number.

"She does not stay long with any brigade," the Party organizer Iakubova explained. "Although she is not a bad worker, each brigade tries to get rid of her. After all, all of them are struggling to get the distinction of a brigade of Communist labor. Now, can a member of such a brigade be weaving the material for God?"

The shift ended. The crowd moved toward the exit. People walked in lively conversation. In the distance, separated from others, hurriedly, not even glancing aside, a lonely figure walked in the mud. This was Brydnia. . . .

It is your fault, your neglect, comrades of the "Kamvolnii" factory combine, that Eudokiia, being twenty-two years of age, turned into a renegade.

Do you remember how she entered school as a little girl? She progressed like others, and even joined the *Komsomol*, like others. Then, talk like this started:

"I am going to marry only the man whom the presbyter chooses for me."

"But you are so pretty, and the groom might be squint-eyed or freckled [pockmarked]," her girl friends teased her.

"Apparently such would be God's will."

People merely laughed and shook their heads: what strange ideas this girl has . . .

Yes, now matters are too far advanced and it will be much more difficult to make Brydnia return to the right way.

Now about Arkhip Lazarev. In order to learn his story, I went to Spokoinaia Stanitsa, the center of the Spokoinenskii Region. I visited the Regional Party Committee.

"How could it happen that, so close to you, at Stanitsa Nadezhnaia, Arkhip Lazarev has been sitting in chains?" I asked the Secretary of the Regional Committee, Anna Avraanivba Kurgan.

"Maybe, he had been sitting there for ten years," the secretary replied wryly. "But we learned about it only a month ago when we read about it in the local paper."

About fifteen kilometers away from Spokoinaia, there is Nadezhnaia Stanica. By the woods, on the steep bank of the river, there stands the house in which the Lazarevs live. It stands there away from all the other houses, somehow resembling its owner who during the war was a German policeman and in peacetime, remained an individual peasant. One window in the house is tightly closed by shutters. A narrow path leads to the abode of the leader of the sectarians of Nadezhnaia.

Our approach was met with the mad barking of a dog; strangers were approaching. The owner of the house met us with distrust. Hesitantly, he asked us to come in.

The house was divided into two parts. In one of them, a kind of private church was built: an iconostasis [a partition on which icons are placed], burning sanctuary lamps, Communion bread and a self-made, miniature "God's grave." An icon of the Mother of God took the central place. I recognized it right away after the description I saw in the "Atheist's Guide": it was the same icon on which, at the order of the Tsarist satrap, Arakcheyev, was painted his love, Minkina, as a model. Now, *people come to pray to this icon.*

It was half-dark behind the wooden partition. The window was tightly closed. It was here, on a wooden floor covered with torn rags, that "God's servant," Arkhip, has passed ten years of his life, chained by his leg.

Arkhip was only seven years old when his mother and his older sister—both religious fanatics—started to perform religious rites with the child. The boy was scared, cried, asked to be left alone. But they continued. They even started to "treat" him for illness. They would put a basin filled with water on his head and pour melted wax into the water with prayers accompanying the procedure. Naturally, such "procedures" caused nervous disorders in the boy.

He would escape to the woods. They would catch him and continue to "cure" him. He started crying in his sleep and getting scared of other people. And the Lazarevs decided: "Since his illness is pleasing to God, it shows that his is God's choice." A very simple and cruel approach: disabled people, and, especially those with nervous disorders, enjoy special respect on the part of "true, orthodox Christians" to which the Lazarevs claim to belong. In order to make "God's choice" submit to God's will without opposing it, he was put in chains. After that, he first forgot how to read and write, then ceased to speak and understand.

He sits in front of us, a lost man of twenty-six. The expression of his face is dull and thoughtless; his dimmed eyes fix on one spot. He could never play with the village boys of his age. He would never enter the agricultural institute, the way Iuri Kharchenko did; he would never become a physician, like Aleksie Samonenko, or return to his native *sovkhoz* [state farm] as an engineer, like Dmitrii Bygolevskii. . . .

"Yet the case of Arkhip is an exceptional one," Comrade Kurgan assures me. "And, in general, we had, during the past year, 2,106 lectures given and this, mind you, with only 2,000 planned. Of this number, sixty-five were anti-religious ones."

Apparently, the leaders of Spokoinenskii Region are satisfied in their minds. But, *do people like the parents of Arkhip Lazarev, or Bondarenko, or Malashein, or other members of the sect attend such lectures?* You, Comrade Kurgan, say that "in reality there is no sect, just a few old people praying quietly." Quietly, indeed? And do you know what propaganda and agitation these "quiet" people are engaged in? How *they distribute anti-Soviet literature?* How they threatened one of the local residents, Mrs. L . . . demanding that she sacrifice to God her daughter Raia? It is true, Mrs. L's daughter is not in danger any more. But it was not you, comrades, who helped her: Raia left, or rather escaped from the settlement, and lives in a city now.

Now, finally, a criminal case against the Lazarevs is in progress; they eventually saw it as wise to spread the version that their son was mentally retarded and they started healing him. After ten years, the unhappy boy was unchained. They want to take him to the hospital. But will they? This is not yet known because, you see, a parental agreement is required for such action. And the parents do not agree.

What to do, when the obscurantists ruin human life "given by God." Are we sure that little Iasha Stepaniuga will not share Arkhip Lazarev's fate? These were my uneasy thoughts when I was leaving the settlement.

At Armavira I got the answer to my question. Two sisters were admitted to the local children's home: *Nina and Luda Berdarev. They were taken away from their mother on the basis of a Court decision:* the woman fanatic had forbidden her children to attend school. In vain the headmaster and the teachers tried to make the sectarian understand her duties. Then, the Village Council of Ilin turned to the Court. The Court decided that the defendant performed her powers with detriment to the children, and deprived her of her parental rights.

The *sisters came to the children's home* without a smile on their tense faces. *They prayed, crossed themselves, whispered.* The girls were not bothered by special talks or inquiries. Life in the children's home took its normal course. The children studied, worked in shops, went for excursions, watched television, attended Pioneer meetings. The house on the Lermontovskaia Street was visited by old, moustached trustees or by young girls from the rail plant. Now, Nina, for the first time in her life, goes to a movie theater and does not cover her eyes, and watches *The Cheated One*. Then she tells her instructor: "I liked it very much."

I noticed how happy Nina is now, how eagerly she reads and how gladly she studies. Luda has not yet recovered completely, but, surely, she will become like her sister. And again, I thought of little Iasha Stepaniuga. I visited him at home. On the gate, there was a sign: "Vicious dog in the yard." I hope the readers will forgive me for the comparison: Iasha's mother looked to me more vicious. Lidia Ivanovna immediately attacked me:

"Why do I not let them go to the movies? But this is a devil's pleasure, that's why. I destroyed the radio receiver, too. I am myself illiterate and, as you see, I live." With pleasure, she looks at her good, new house. *"My husband and I are believing people; therefore, our children will not wear Pioneer scarves. . . ."*

The married couple Stepaniuga—are staunch sectarians. They have seven children—seven small Soviet citizens who are forced to live behind tightly closed shutters, separating them from the world. The bad will of their obscurantist parents may even deprive them of their right to learning which has become binding law for all children of our country. Would it not be better for the children of such people as the Stepaniugas to live in big houses with large windows through which the sun and the sky and the green grass could be seen, perhaps in a house like the one in which Nina and Luda now live?

Alla Trubnikova,
Special correspondent of *Ogoniok*

Source: *Kazakhstanskaia Pravda,* January 31, 1962

7

End to the Obscurantists

From the Courtroom:
   The camera men of the television studio of Karaganda succeeded in photographing a few unusual scenes: In a small room, people are kneeling and, in a singing voice, shout incomprehensible invocations. Soon, *they get into ecstasy,* start shaking faster and faster until, finally, some of them faint. This is the praying exercise of the "Christians of the Evangelic Faith," or, as they are called, the *Piatidesiatniki.*
   During the past years, this illegal sect spread in Karaganda and got under its influence about two hundred people. The sectarians started interfering in family lives of the working people and recruiting new members everywhere it was possible.
   The disease spread. Executive Committees of regional Councils and the workers' deputies and other social organizations received dozens of petitions from citizens requesting that they be protected against the infringement by the

sectarians and that the activities of the obscurantists be curbed. *As a result, a criminal trial got under way against the leaders of the sect.*

For five days, a show trial against the *"pastors," the human soul hunters,* was in progress in the Karaganda Cultural Palace of the miners. It aroused enormous interest in the working people of the city.

Who are these sect leaders, so highly skilled in invading human souls? Here is the "presbyter" of the community, Afanazii Drobkov, a skinny man with a thin, Jesuit-type mouth, a sharp nose and an oily voice. He has a special secondary education. He used to be a teacher and taught Physics and Mathematics during the war, he was taken prisoner and recruited by the German Intelligence. "For diligence," he was given the rank of a private first class in Hitler's Army, and awarded a bronze medal. For this treason, he was sentenced to ten years in prison. *After serving his time, he settled in Karaganda and undertook to organize the sect of the* Piatidesiatniki, *in which he took the post of the Head.*

And here is Geronim Domanskii, *a sinister figure of a fanatic, author of numerous psalms and sermons* which are characterized by his hatred of Soviet people. *Some time ago, he was sentenced* for anti-Soviet activity. *He served his time and came to Karaganda where he became a deacon of the community.*

Wriggling and playing the fool, the third defendant, "regent" Fedor Borovikov, gives his testimony. *Twelve years ago, he was sentenced; he then came to Karaganda and became an active member of the sect.*

Skillfully managing the believers, these leaders subjected the whole sect to their will. *They taught that "God should take first place in our thoughts, feelings and deeds."* They tried to convince the believers that everything that existed outside of their community, was "sinful." *One should, they insisted, stay away from worldly vanity. The earthly life is only a temporary existence—a true life only will come after death, in heaven.*

Everything in the sectarians is directed toward destroying in the human being the faith in his own powers, toward a pessimistic conception of reality and, eventually, toward turning man into a weak-willed slave.

We must not forget that the sect of the Pentecostals came into existence in 1907 in the U.S.A. The introduction of this sect in our country was the result of the work of American preachers who, some forty years ago, started their religious offensive by advancing the slogan: "America and Russia for Christ." In respect to all Soviet matters, the sect took a clearly hostile position. It is evident that the residents of Karaganda were not inclined to tolerate the fact that the sect leaders educate the believers in hatred toward the Soviet system and advance religion against the bright ideas of our society.

Thirty-two witnesses appeared before the Court. Many of them angrily told the Court about the lies and hypocrisy of the sectarian preachers, of the fact that they entangled honest Soviet people by dominating their souls. It was difficult to listen without indignation to the testimony of the worker of mine No. 38, *Timofel Ursu, the locksmith of "T.E.T.s," Michael Schchegol, whose families were destroyed by the sectarians*, of the retired worker F. F. Chupretova, of the worker of mine No. 37, Mrs. Elizaveta Novikova, of the manager of mine No. 38, Michael Grebenshchikov, the leader Veniamin Shmunk and others. All of them violently accused the sectarians.

But there were also witnesses, who, raising their eyes toward the ceiling, invoked God, incomprehensibly mumbled something about conscience, about brother and sister in faith. These were the members of the sect. They surprisingly resembled each other—pale, tired faces.

Aleksei Kirko, a dirty-looking man not young any more. *He is an ardent fanatic.* "One finds what one seeks," Kirko maintains. It is easy to find what Kirko is seeking in life. It was not an accident that *such reactionary magazines as The Peacemaker Will Come*, published still in the "lordly" Poland [pre-war Poland] and full of libelous attacks against the young Soviet Republic, *were kept in his home*.

And here, again, is Ivan Run, plasterer in mine No. 70. He doesn't know even who Iuri Gagarin is: he is not familiar with the achievements of Soviet science and technology.

The appearance of *Mrs. Neonila Krechmarovskaia* makes a distressing impression. She *came to Karaganda only one year ago and immediately fell into the dragnet of the sectarians. Maria Pliska, who met her, suggested that she stayed in her apartment without payment. There the meetings of the sectarians took place often. Krechmarovs-*

kaia started taking part in these meetings. Now she is a downtrodden, poisoned woman.

Those present at the trial were virtually shocked by the evidence given in testimony by the headmaster of tⱨ school No. 23 [Mrs.] E. G. Milevskaia. She told the story of the hard life of the children of sectarians who attend her school. One is Liuda Domanskaia. Like other children, she wears a Pioneer scarf around her neck. *Liuda is an exemplary student,* jokes with her girl friends, laughs, plays during recess. But, when the end of the school hours approach a shadow comes over her face. The girl becomes uncommunicative, nervous, angry. When the last bell rings, Liuda takes down her scarf and stoops and steals out of the room. Her other life begins, a forced, gloomy life of the daughter of a sectarian.

During the trial, many examples of suffering were described, by *people who believed that "God's grace" comes as a result of praying.* Such "grace" came also down on Anna Bavalennaia. The sectarians used the occasion of her husband's illness and advised her to seek solace in prayers. During one of the sermons, Anna heard that even God's will can be tested ... and she made up her mind. *When, after the prayers, she came out on the street, holding her six-year-old son in her arms, she threw herself on the ground in front of a passing truck.* Fortunately, the driver noticed her in time and stopped. Anna was not hurt.

The preachers triumphed:

"You see," they said, "God did not let you die. His will was done."

Then Anna threw herself in front of a train. Her son was hurt and she passed away in terrible pain.

Also the plight of Michael Shchegol was described at the trial. *While he was in service, the sectarians entangled his wife in their nets, and moved her from the Crimea to Karaganda. There Michael found her, completely changed.*

The list of the crimes of the sectarians is a long one. The Community Prosecutor, lecturer in Philosophy at the technological institute, [Mrs.] A. G. Arkhipova, talked about them with indignation. *Doctor of Sciences, an expert in Forensic Medicine, Professor M. A. Sviadoshch, convincingly proved the harm done by these praying sessions.* The concluding statement of the Prosecutor, P. G. Grachkov, sounded angry.

The trial clearly showed the malicious nature of the

sectarian teaching. In front of the spectators scandalous facts of scoffing young people and children were presented in a long row.

It was proven in the course of the trial that Drobkov, Domanskii and Borovikov violated Soviet laws by organizing an illegal sect. They conducted secret meetings of the sectarians. All these acts are punishable under Section 200 of the Criminal Code of the Kazakh S.S.R. So, those attending the trial met the just sentence with approval.

The Judges of the District Court sentenced A. N. Drobkov and G. C. Domanskii to five years, and F. G. Borovikov to three years in prison.

It should be added that *the Party and* Komsomol *organization of Karaganda wage a rather weak fight against the sectarians.* No party of *Komsomol* were present at the trial. *The ground under the feet of the obscurantists and fanatics is not yet hot enough in the city.* Naturally, *their activities cannot be curbed by one trial, even a very sensational one.* An everyday, persistent, educational-atheistic propaganda work must be conducted in order to save from the clutches of the sectarians those whom the *preachers, the inveterate catches of human souls,* have succeeded in bluffing.

City of Karaganda
V. Grigoriev

Source: *Kazakhstanskaia Pravda,* May 17, 1962

8

To Fight with Reason Rather than with "Records"

Recently, one of the leaders of the local sect of the Evangelical Christian Baptists, I. F. Koroliuk, was on trial at Shchuchinsk. For many years he had preached sectarian dogmas, distributed religious literature and dragged into the sect unsteady people, especially children.

The People's Court, consistently, step by step, unmasked the antisocial activities of Koroliuk, and showed the harm which he caused to the Communist education of the working people. The witnesses angrily accused the *"brother in Christ."*

"My daughter, Nadezhda, was only sixteen years of age when she got under the influence of Koroliuk," Mrs. T. Moiseeva declared. "Until then, the girl was happy, but then she grew sad, became secretive and in conversation with me, once she started talking some nonsense, such as: *'I am not living here, I am merely existing, the true life will come in the other world.'* This is what this 'God's righteous man' taught her."

R. Cura: "My brother's wife, Tatiana, did not return home for several days. It came out later that she was caught in a sticky snare, cunningly prepared by Koroliuk. On this basis, scandals occurred in the family."

Important evidence was given by the witnesses Prusskaia, Iushchitsina and Val. *They all told how Koroliuk, like a spider, spread his web in order to catch his next victim.*

The People's Court passed a just decision which was met with approval by the residents of the town.

Naturally, we could put a period and stop here, were it not for one circumstance. *Many people in the town and its vicinity are still engulfed in the cloud of the sectarian nonsense.* One should help them to come out of it on the wide road of life.

Well, how was the existence of the sect at Shchuchinsk made possible? How is the atheistic propaganda organized there, what is the real impact it exerts on the believers?

The Regional Party Committee and many local Party organizations take a pacifying attitude toward the churchmen and sectarians; they do not carry on a vigorous, offensive atheistic propaganda. At times, the situation assumes curious forms.

In some settlements of the Urumkai *sovkhoz* the sectarians are active without obstacles, they harm the souls of the people and hamper the collective in its work. Comrade Kozakov, an atheist lecturer, suggested to the members of the Party Committee that they make a few talks to the farmers and cattle breeders. He personally appeared also in the village of Dmitreevka. *After the lecture, he visited the home of the Secretary of the Party organization of that department, Comrade Marus and, to his amazement, he saw an icon in the room.* Marus hurriedly explained: his old mother still prayed; therefore, out of respect to her, they still keep this attribute of the past.

There are in the region some Communists in whose homes religious rites are held.

The inveterate sectarian, Blank, worked for a long time as a lecturer in the eight-year school No. 2; P. M. Nikolaeva lectured in the upper grades of the 30th Railroad School and, in addition . . . she sang in the Church choir. The teachers of these schools, among them many Communists, passed by these facts indifferently. After long deliberations, the office of the Regional Party Committee finally put on the order of the day the question of the status and ways of improvement of the educational atheistic work in the region. It was decided: to increase the atheistic work among the believers, to create permanent groups of atheist agitators with the local Party organizations, etc. However, three months have passed since that decision has been made and the situation of the antireligious propaganda remains unchanged.

"There are sectarians in our collective," says Comrade Kolbasiuk, Deputy Secretary of the local Party organization in the furniture plant. "We work on them, we read lectures. . . ."

The Secretary of the Party organization of the glass factory reports: "I have not received the decision of the Regional Party Office, but still, in the course of this year we had three lectures read on educational-atheistic topics. We have free movies that show the harm done by religion."

Again and again the same thing. Lectures, movies, care for a good "Record" . . . Obviously, at Shchuchinsk they do not want to understand that lectures alone do not suffice. What is needed is persistent individual work. Only then the atheistic propaganda can be successful.

The main reason which prevents the needed individual work with the believers from expanding is rooted in the formalistic, bureaucratic attitude of some Party organization leaders to this important matter. It is easy to establish how many antireligious lectures were read and how many people (no matter—believers or not) have heard them. It is also easy to present in figures (whose accuracy is always a relative one) other measures which were undertaken. If the worst comes to the worst, one can be satisfied with a simple earmark in the report.

But how can such a delicate psychological matter as the effect of an atheist's work be expressed on paper? What figures can be used to express the conquest of the soul of a believer?

Success can only come when the job is done not for the record's sake.

V. Naumov

Source: *Sovetskaia Rossiia,* May 23, 1962

9

God's Fools in Christ

From the Courtroom:

Those present in the courtroom were laughing aloud. Contrary to the custom, the judges also smiled. It was obviously an absurdity that *those sitting in the dock, leaders of the sect of the* Piatidesiatniki *were regarded by their flock as those seeking the truth and by some even as "saints."* Now these "Father Saints" were replying to the questions of the chairman of the Court:

"Say, Garbuzov, it is said that you have seen Jesus Christ alive. Is it true?"

"There was such a vision," Viktor replies shyly. "I looked and saw Him coming out of the fire house and walking around on the factory courtyard, even the flap of His robe was open. I rubbed my eyes, but He kept walking on."

"Did you talk to Him?"

"Well, no, I had no chance. . . ."

Yes, all this looks ridiculous at this moment, when there are hundreds of people present in the courtroom, when the room is brightly lit by electric lights. *But the sect of the* Piatidesiatniki *operates in the dark since it went underground.* Vladimir and Viktor Garbuzov were not on trial because they were believers. There is no persecution for religious beliefs in our country. The Garbuzov brothers are on trial charged with antisocial activities which were harmful both to the country and to those who happened to be caught in the snare of the sect.

The Piatidesiatniki *are an awfully reactionary sect.* It is harmful, first of all, to the rank and file members of the community, the naïve and simple people who really trust these charlatans. Their rites are savagely cruel. Those who are uninitiated can hardly imagine the so-called ceremony of baptism with the Holy Spirit. It is something wild, senseless and cruel. *People kneel down and bring themselves to ecstasy.*

A witness, S. E. Marchenkov, testified in Court:

"I happened to come into the house of the *kolkhoz* member, Mrs. Kotikova. I did not know that the *Piatidesiatniki* Baptists assemble in her house, and I unexpectedly came there during the high moment of their prayers. A terrible scene presented itself to my eyes. *One of the praying women was singing psalms, others tore their hair, still others writhed in cramps on the floor,* scratched the boards with their fingernails, hit the floor with their heads, *shouted, laughed and cried.* I automatically tiptoed back and left the room."

There is no wonder that many cannot stand such trials; they get sick mentally and with other illnesses, and become invalids.

The spiritual pastors try many ways to enslave their "brothers" and "sisters." The members of the sect are forbidden to attend movies, listen to the radio and to read newspapers. The pastors declare all these things as devilish occupations.

The Garbuzovs themselves, however, did not shun the fruits of civilization. They bought a motorcycle, a television set, a radio receiver and a tape recorder. *As a matter of fact, the radio receiver was used by them to listen to libelous programs from abroad, and with the aid of the tape recorder, they recorded psalms of their own creation.*

The sectarians are especially eager in hunting for youth and engage in criminal activities by making the minors

*compose and distribute "holy" writings which always have
reactionary contents.*

"I am a mother and I wish all children happiness," a
witness, Mrs. I. A. Nikolaieva, who was a member of the
sect for a long time, stated in the Court. "I ask you, citizen
judges, isolate these *monsters,* protect innocent children! If
you only knew how cruelly, how pitilessly they wound the
souls of the children. I'll tell you about the tragedy of one
Vania Podeshchenkov. The Garbuzovs lured him into the
sect when he was still a minor. *With his whole heart, he
trusted their insidious speeches and believed that one could
merit God's graces by the way of great zeal.* I personally
witnessed how this baptism of the Holy Spirit was carried
out. Vania kneeled for a long time, read prayers and
bowed. He hit the floor with his forehead, shouted and
cried. Sweat poured down from his body, his hair was
tousled, his looks were wild. Finally, the powerless young-
ster was picked up and carried away hardly alive. After
that, he nearly lost his mind."

The audience kept silent, shocked by the testimony of
the witnesses. But all burst into prolonged and sincere
applause when the judge read the verdict. *Vladimir Garbuzov was sentenced to five years and Viktor Garbuzov to
three years in prison.*

Roslavl, Province of Smolensk
Dm. Osipov, Our correspondent

Source: *Izvestiia,* July 5, 1962

10

The Obscurantist

From the Courtroom:
In the settlement "The Red Builder" (*Krasnii Stroitel*),
there worked as a driver for the management of the

commercial transport *Mosgorispolkom* one I. F. Ovsianni-kov. *During the past year, he joined the old-rite religious community,* started drinking and behaving like a hooligan.

As a father, he forced his small children Vera and Boris to pray, wear crosses and forbade them to join the youth organizations of *Oktabriata* and Pioneers. For disobedience, he banged their heads on the floor, made them kneel in front of the icons, he offended them with indecent words and threw them out of the house. When the mother tried to protect the children, Ovsiannikov beat her up and poured boiling water on her.

The People's Court had sentenced Ovsiannikov to eight years of forced labor in the fall of 1961. Yet he did not stop taunting his children and his wife. As a result of continual beatings and persecutions, his daughter Vera was hospitalized.

Now, Ovsiannikov received a just reward for his fanaticism: The People's Court of the Moskvoretskii Region sentenced him to three years in prison. The Moscow City Court rejected the appeal. The Court, by a special decision, drew the attention of the social organizations to their weak antireligious activity among the population of the settlement.

M. Barkovskii,
Member of the Moscow City Court

Source: *Sovetskaia Kirghizia,* August 8, 1962

11

According to their Merits

From the Courtroom:

Iakov Peters is fifty-six years of age. Residing in the Ivanovka Station of the Chuiskii Region, he headed, since 1960, the sect of the Evangelical Christian Baptists. It is known that the Baptists forbid their sect members to attend movies, theaters and clubs, listen to the radio, to watch T.V. programs or to take part in the activities of community organizations. They are trying to bar their children from the influence of the school and the Pioneers, and they forbid them to participate in the circles of artistic self-activities and in sporting teams.

For the infringement upon the civil rights of Soviet people, Peters was made to face criminal responsibility.

Recently, the assizes of the Chuiskii People's Court, with the participation of the Community Prosecutor, tried the case against Peters in the hall of the factory club. Peters was sentenced to four years in prison with confinement in a camp of correctional labor. Those present viewed the sentence with great approval.

V. Kim,
Assistant Prosecutor of the Chuiskii Region,
Junior Counsellor of Justice

Source: *Kazakhstanskaia Pravda,* September 12, 1962

12

Fanatics on Trial

A criminal trial against the leaders of an illegal Baptist community, operating in the Zaton District of the city, came to a close here.

Here is what the young witness, a Pioneer girl, Vera Arent, told the Court:

"Uncle Asaf and Aunt Erika visited us on the occasion of the New Year tree (celebration). Nobody recognized them. The uncle was dressed in sheepskin inside out, and a big iron chain clanged in his hand, and the aunt was all in white with a terrible mask on her face.

"Pray, children," they shouted. "We are going to put in chains those who refuse to pray, and put them to death."

" 'Death'—Aunt Erika whipped our legs with switches and made us kneel down."

The girl told in detail about the horrors that existed in the house of the Arents and other Baptist families. The leaders of the sect tried, by force, to make minor children join in the secret prayers of the sectarians. They forbade the children to visit movies, concerts, engage in sports, and told the Pioneers to take off their red scarves.

The trial lasted for three days. Many witnesses testified and completely exposed the fanaticism of the sectarians. The Court sentenced the leaders of the sect to various terms in prison. The Baptists V. Krivosheev and V. Rudnev were deprived of parental rights.

Semipalatinsk
V. Zakharov,
Correspondent of Kasakh Telegr. Agency

Source: *Komsomolskaia Pravda,* September 25, 1962

13

During the Trial Intermission

(Notes of an Atheist)

Recently, I attended a trial session in the criminal case against the leader of the sect of the *Piatidesiatniki,* Leonid Shevchenko. Every time I entered the courtroom one particular contrast would strike me. The people of Krasnoiarsk are usually exceptionally healthy—physically and mentally. In the room, all the faces are fresh, rosy—what we call "blood and milk." On the other hand, in the docks in the corners of the room, I saw black clothing, sallow complexions, sunken eyes, cheerless young men with their heads shaven, girls with their heads covered with scarves in the fashion of old women. Sectarians. Like dead grass withered in the spring. This is not an accidental contrast and not only an outward one. *The tiredness of the sectarians is the result of their nightly "zealotry," unnatural rites and exhausting prayers.*

It was not the first time that I met sectarians, attempting to snatch my friends out of their claws. But, at this trial, the stink and dirt of this little world opened to me with their full strength.

When you look for a word best suited to express the "program" of the *Piatidesiatniki,* you will find in it—hostility. Hostility, reaction, hatred of humanity. The leaders of the sect forbid their members everything "secular," i.e. everything that is ours, Soviet: books, radio, the Pioneer scarf, participation in social activities. Even the joining of a Labor Union is declared to be a godless thing.

The sects are hostile to everything that is bright and good in man. All talks about sympathy, sharing and plenty of love which, allegedly, exist in their midst—are nothing else but fairy tales.

Once, on a narrow path across the frozen river of Kachu, I met the preacher Elena Puchinskaia. We started to talk, cautiously, ready to counter any caustic remark. Suddenly, my three-year-old son ran over the ice toward the opening. I ran after him, caught him into my arms, but the ice crashed under me. I managed to get out of the hole holding my son over my head, but then fell into another opening. The banks of the river were empty. I only saw the silhouette of the sectarian on the path. She did not bother to come to my help or to call people. She silently watched me. Perhaps it was anger that added to my strength. I got out and, wet with my terrified son in my hands, I went home. And the preacher called after me:

"This is a sign."

Yet they have sufficient "sympathy" to fawn a person in distress and to catch him in their spider web. Then the "man-hating" zealotries follow.

"Even if you know, very well, all the wild, immoral and inhuman character of the sect, you have a hard time answering questions like this: *Why is it that the sectarians still find new partisans? Where do they get their strength from?* An assembly of fanatical, half-illiterate old women. . . . And, among them, Lelia Bordysheva, a sickly, secretive girl, Nadezhda Davidova, a young woman not yet deprived of her charm, who not long ago graduated from the Pedagogical Institute of Krasnoiarsk. . . . What was it that attracted them to Leonid Shevchenko, to Elena Puchinskaia?

I do not hesitate to reply for myself: *it was determination and activity of the soul catchers. We usually imagine our ideological foes either as mentally retarded or as moneygrabbers whose only aim is to profit from those fooled by them.*

But Shevchenko is an engineer by education, strong, smart and diabolically shrewd. Earlier, he was three times sentenced for anti-Soviet activities. Apparently, he recognized that his open hostile activity would not find anybody's support, he started acting under the mask of a priest. Being experienced, knowing Psychology, having mastered the ways of conspiracy, Shevchenko easily adjusted himself to the sectarian environment and later became the sect's leader.

He would go from house to house, getting to know the sectarian families, looking for unstable people whom he tried to convert to his sect either personally or through his helpers. He knew how to help people to get a job, or to give efficient practical advice. *Kindness* and threat, *material support* and blackmail, *humble plea* and preaching in rage—these were the tools which Shevchenko mastered completely.

The witnesses told about broken families, about women who wound up in mental institutions, about children with their souls harmed. *People, "doped" by Shevchenko and his assistants, refused to fulfill their citizen's duties, tore off their Pioneer scarves, trampled the red flag with their shoes.*

How much time and energy was used to create so much evil!

And what was it that we, the activists, the Komsomol members did in opposition to this strategy and skillful tactics of the sectarians?

Well, practically—nothing. Judge for yourselves: in all Krasnoiarsk, a city of half a million inhabitants, there is only one more or less active group of Komsomol members —atheists, consisting of fifteen students. But even they have little training in the art of convincing, the difficult job of dealing with those gone astray.

Now what about those gone astray? We don't even know

how to help a man who entered on the pathway of cooperation with religion. The pious aunt told Vala N.: "You are not going to enroll in the Institute: The teacher is against God!" Vala did not follow the order. But this is as far as she was able to go. In the home of her aunt the sectarians would meet as before. Now how did the schoolmate of Vala help her, the *Komsomol* member, how did they support her weakening will to fight? In no way at all.

Gena Kulikov's mother forced him to pray, beat him, locked him up in the storeroom. The boy starved, suffered humiliation, but would not give in. He escaped from home and started a life of a homeless. And we, the atheists, to our shame, did not even know about this unequal struggle.

Our forces are scattered, not united by a common front line connecting teachers and parents, propagandists and *Komsomol* workers. In the *Komsomol* environment, they don't even consider it a major neglect when an activist does not conduct any antireligious work and doesn't even know it. I knew many facts which made me worry. *I knew that several* Komsomol *members fell under the influence of religious people,* and I went to the Central regional committee of the V.L.K.S.M. [Leninist Young Communist League of the Soviet Union], hoping that this agency would finally turn its interest toward atheistic work. But we did not get beyond talking.

It cannot be excused or even understood that, in the City Committee of the Communist Youth, not a single person is busy with the atheist work or prepares young people for this job. Why this indifference, such inactivity among the *Komsomol* leaders? They ask persistently for waste paper, for scrap metal, for membership dues. They even give orders [to collect these items and dues]. But it does not cause them any headache that people get lost, that through *sectarian channels, hostile ideology penetrates into* our midst, along with wild habits. We cannot rely only on the essential influence of our basically very healthy Soviet environment. Even the greenest meadow is not secure from rotten grass. We should act in such a way that the forces of the healthy environment lend their support to the work we started and kill the roots of malicious thistle.

Krasnoiarsk
I. Voevodin,
Chairman of the Club of Atheists

Source: *Turkmenskaia Iskra,* October 7, 1962

14

The Sentence Was Met with Approval

One late evening in July the residents of Belinskii Street were awakened from their sleep by shrill cries. When they ran out to the street they saw near one house a group of people who tried to pick up from the ground a woman shaken by hysterics.

"Another job of these damned sectarians. When will they be taken under control," a tall, elderly man said gloomily. It was suggested that an ambulance should be called.

"She does not need any doctors. Our sister in Christ was visited by God's grace; she talks with Him," a present sectarian said in an oily voice. The woman was picked up and carried into a house.

Six neat houses were situated on one side of Belinskii Street. Over high fences one could see bright white walls covered with climbing vine. Houses like any other ordinary ones. It is difficult to believe that, inside, a disgusting sect of fanatics, the *Piatidesiatniki* made its nest.

Three times weekly, at night, trying not to catch the eyes of the passersby, "brothers" and "sisters" sneak in here. Some bring children with them. Quietly the gate creaks.

Gradually, the little room becomes crowded. Its windows are tightly covered by heavy curtains.

All kneel down. One of the leaders of the sect starts to read the gospel in a monotonous, dull voice. Those present repeat after him. The murmur, initially hardly heard, becomes louder and louder.

Then the so-called *proritsatel* [augur] of the sect, Podolskii, a big man of forty-three, starts his sermon.

The essence of his sermon is always the same. He accuses the believers of not conscientiously following the "Holy Scriptures," of aiming at worldly things, threatens with all possible heavenly punishments that await those who would attend movies, theaters, read newspapers or books and take part in community life. His voice rises to a scream.

It is terrifying to look at this picture from outside. In the stuffy, tightly covered room, hysterical cries and shouts are heard; people are shaking and hitting the floor. According to the assertions of the leaders, it is exactly at such moments that "God" descends upon them. With their eyes wide open from horror, terrified children watch their shouting parents.

The zeal causes psychological disorder in people and hurts them morally and physically. At times, it has a tragic effect. One cannot read without deep compassion the letter from Anisia Zakharovna Flinta, full of extreme sorrow.

Her husband who came to Mary in 1960, fell under the influence of *Piatidesiatniki*. Having regularly attended their meetings, he eventually ruined his nervous system, became insane and died. His wife remained alone with seven minor children. "May they be damned, those fanatics who took away the father of the children and my husband," Anisia Flinta writes.

With Jesuit-like cunningness and disloyalty, smartly taking advantage of the slightest difficulties of the people, the Piatidesiatniki *managed to draw them into their nets. For example, they found out that Evdokiia Kirichenko was left alone after her husband's death and was frequently ill. They arranged to visit her at her home. They pretended to sympathize with her and comfort her;* making reference to the "will of God" they gradually managed to convince her that one can get rid of a sickness only through prayers. Evdokiia started to attend their meetings, but the more fervently she prayed the worse she fared healthwise. In addition, *the sectarians started to drag into the sect her daughter Galina.* After a few senseless prayer exercises, the latter, too, was not feeling well. Then, Kirichenko realized into what abyss the *Piatidesiatniki* had dragged her, and she broke with them. The seamstress of the Krupskaia factory, Lidiia Muliar, and the young worker Nadeshda Nekrasova also left the sect.

Well, and what happened to the gay and lovely girl, Liza Lapiichuk, the mail carrier of the local communication office?

In a short time, she became tired, sickly and irritable. One could hardly believe that she was only twenty-two years of age. *Liza is zealous in her prayers and rejects all earthly joys.*

A killer physically destroys a man. The Pentecostals destroy him morally. It is children who suffer most. *Aleksander, the son of Razdaigora, one of the most ardent fanatics of the sect,* is fifteen years of age, but he has read only one book, has never been to the movies; instead, he *every day,* at the parent's insistence, *reads aloud the Holy Scripture.* Anatolii, twelve, the son of the leader of the sect, Gonchar, attends the fourth grade. He is a poor student, does not associate with anybody, does not attend evening meetings at school.

The sectarians claim that they have no leaders, that they are all equal under God. But this is not so. There are leaders, all right. It was they who, by cunning and lies, have dragged into their spider web unwise, uneducated, unstable people. The moral image of these "spiritual pastors" is disgusting and loathsome. Here is one of them— Sergei Moroz. He is not yet forty years of age. During the difficult years of the "Fatherland War" while a member of the Soviet Army, he betrayed his country. The Soviet Government showed true humanity in treating him and conditionally set him free from jail.

Also other leaders of the Pentecostals spent years in prisons, such as the sectarian presbyter, Ivan Gonchar, and Fedor Velsh. Also the augur of the sect, Podolskii, managed to avoid being drafted into the Soviet Army, by presenting all kinds of certificates.

At present, they besmirch everything around them. Their sermons are full of lies and hypocrisy, from the beginning to the end. Calling upon the sect members, in the name of God, to practice moderation and abstinence, *they themselves turned during their lives into grabbers and money-grubbers.* They have all solid, big homes surrounded by high stone walls, orchards, beehives and many other valuable things. Having imposed upon the people, they receive monthly dues in the form of so-called donations for God, they have never given any account to the believers as to how this money is being spent. The wives of the leaders, while taking no part in any useful community work, are quite busy tailoring at home and then selling their products at speculative prices on the market. Ivan Gonchar, who works at the building department of the trust *Turkmengi-*

drostroi, systematically brings home from there boards, sheetiron and other materials. Podolskii privately works as a carpenter at collective farms charging extremely high prices. In order to conceal traces, he registered the big house which he bought with the proceeds in the name of the sister of his wife, Solomiia Kuziak.

"God forbids beating women," the leaders of the sect say hypocritically. At the same time, one of them, Sergei Moroz, systematically ridicules his wife. When this became widely known, "presbyter" Gonchar gave him utterly unholy advice:

"You stupid, you better take her into the storeroom and beat her there, but see to it that no traces are left."

The working people requested that the leaders and inspirers of the fanatical sect be made criminally responsible.

So, now, Ivan Gonchar, Vasilii Podolskii, Sergei Moroz and Fedor Velsh are sitting in the dock. Their shoulders are stooped, their eyes look around frightened.

The big hall of the summer club in the settlement of the builders of the Karakumskii canal is filled. One after another the witnesses appear. Among them are also those who, some time ago, definitely broke away from the Pentecostals, when they recognized the extent of their deprivation and obscurantism. The testimony of the witnesses completely unmasked the savage and fanatical activity of the sect. The treatment of the children by the Pentecostals made the workers especially indignant. When it was described, the audience reacted with angry shouts:

"Villains, wild fanatics, rascals!"

The heads of the defendants bow lower and lower. Nothing in the world would make them look into the hundreds of angry and condemning eyes.

When Gonchar is asked how he would react to the Court's decision depriving him of his parental power, he looks up and whispers indifferently:

"All according to God's will: apparently this is what He wants."

The concluding statement of the community prosecutor, the master workman of the building department of the trust *Turkmengidrostroi,* Comrade Ivanov!

"We cannot tolerate any more the criminal activities of the leaders of this fanatical sect. They cripple the lives of Soviet people, divert them from productive and creative work, prevent them from building Communism. In the name of the collective of the builders of the Karakumskii canal, we request that these malicious fanatics be isolated."

The People's Court passes a just judgment: the leaders of the sect of the Pentecostals, Conchar, Podolskii, Moroz and Velsh, are sentenced to five years in prison each, with the confiscation of their personal property. Ivan Gonchar is deprived of his parental power.

Those present met this decision with approving applause.

V. Pantiukhin
I. Nudelman

Source: *Kazakhstanskaia Pravda,* December 19, 1962

15

Under the Mask of a "Saint"

From the Courtroom:

Now, after the trial, the pieces of the jigsaw puzzle have been put together. It was established that I. Ie. Grunvald, a native of the Gomel Region, and employee of the Karaganda cloth *combinat* [group of enterprises] near Alma Ata, by means of the abuse of religious prejudices and cheating, engaged in extortion of money from the believers, misappropriated the money and squandered it for drink. Furthermore, *he dragged into the sect of the Baptists his minor son Michael, forbade him to wear his Pioneer scarf,* to attend movies, reply in school to questions on science and chemistry. . . .

It started with little things. Early in 1959, in the worker's settlement, *gossip was spread from house to house:* "A saint," they said, *"appeared at the combinat plant system."*

"Old women are stirring up trouble," the local party and

administration workers decided. "They'll get bored and stop it."

But Grunvald thought differently. Having proclaimed himself a "saint," he started to organize the sect. He found trustful people. *He found a place for secret meetings.* The head of the sect *started inciting the believers to boycott the elections to the People's Courts, to break up mass cultural programs, and he lured children into his sect.* Grunvald behaved in his life scandalously. Five times he married and left his family as soon as children were born. He often threw drinking parties, used dirty language and beat women mercilessly. When he became "saint," he decided to return to his third wife, Marfa, not in order to repent his sins and to help his family, but in order to take away his son.

As long as Misha was with his mother, he was a good pupil, joined the Pioneers, attended the programs of many groups, engaged in sports.

All of a sudden, the boy was literally changed. He started to shun his friends, neglected his homework, *took off his Pioneer scarf.* So it went on. ... At his father's order, the *boy would copy at night various chapters from the Bible, and, during the daytime, distribute the leaflets among the population. In school, he told his superiors:* "*The teachers are lying. Everything on earth was created by God.*"

And Grunvald? While the believers honored him as a "saint," he drank vodka and in a state of drunkenness he blasphemed against God and scolded the Baptists for not contributing enough to the "common purse."

Now, the community, the workers of the court and of the Prosecutor's office decided to tackle the job.

By the decision of the People's Court of the Dzhambul Region, in the Alma Ata province, I. Ie. Grunvald, who was head of the illegal sect of Baptists for four years, was sentenced to three years in prison. He was deprived of his parental power in respect to his son.

This is the whole story of the "saint" rascal. He is in jail. Misha, saved from the hands of the Baptists, again wears the Pioneer scarf.

We could put a period to this story at this point. But I would like to ask these credulous people who continue to gather secretly in dark huts in order to zealously pray to

God: To whom do you entrust your fate, your soul? Whom do you support with your hard-earned rubles?

S. Chestnov

1963

Source: *Pravda Vostoka* (Truth of the East), March 17, 1963

16

The Chairman in the Role of a Hypocrite

From the Courtroom:

At the meeting of the Tashkent Baptists one could often see an elegantly dressed man, with a clean-shaven face and quick-moving eyes. He took a picturesque pose and talked about *"elevated" ideals of baptism, about how good the Baptists were, free from devil, adultery and lies.*

Why, who was this sectarian preacher? A man with two souls and with two families, a man blemished with many serious crimes against the country and the Soviet people.

In 1942, I. N. Volchenko, then living on the territory temporarily occupied by the Fascists, voluntarily became a German policeman. The Fascist faithfully served his masters, helped the persecutors to torture partisans and to rob Soviet citizens. He almost beat to death hungry children who picked corn in the fields or brought some wood from the forests.

At Volchenko's denunciation, many Soviet citizens who fought against the oppressors were shot by the Fascists. When in January 1943 the occupation forces retreated to the West, Volchenko helped them to transport prisoners and the stolen goods.

In 1945 the traitor was arrested and sentenced. But he soon escaped from the prison, managed to get papers in the name of Ivan Josypovich Ivanenko and started advancing to the leadership of the Baptists. He married. Children were born. Neither his wife nor his children knew with what kind of a person they lived.

For a long time, Volchenko-Ivanenko stubbornly tried to win his wife over to the sect of the Baptists. Not being successful, he left his family. He would appear in one or another town as a Baptist preacher. Using the ignorance of the sectarians, he lived at their expense, drinking and leading a dissipated life.

Volchenko-Ivanenko knew that his family had a hard

time supporting itself and that his son was sick. But this did not bother this man of no conscience and honor a bit.

In the prayer houses he read sermons composed by himself, such as: "How many unhappy and poor children do not hear about God." At the same time, naturally he would not disclose his address; to his wife, he wrote: "I am not going to give anything to unbelieving children and God Himself will help me in this. And if you start Court procedure to get alimony, I will escape abroad."

In 1958, residing in the Moscow Community of Evangelical Christian Baptists, Volchenko-Ivanenko met the then Minister of Cultural Affairs of the U.S.A. [sic] Deckford who came to the U.S.S.R. as a tourist. He gave Deckford false "testimony" concerning the situation of the believers in the U.S.S.R. and gave him a Baptist tittle-tattle composed by himself for the use in the "Voice of America."

Soon, the rascal moved to Tashkent. There he easily found common language with the sectarian leaders.

But even the strongest rope can be broken. The criminal was brought to criminal responsibility and sentenced.

It was a just retribution! Let this story make all those who still remain in the nets of similar rascals and obscurantists stop and think.

A. Gorskii

Source: *Sovetskaia Rossiia*, June 9, 1963

17

Six Who Made the Choice

From the Courtroom:

"With whom do you want to live, Liuba?" the Judge asks. "With Mother and Father or with your brother?"

"It is very bad to stay with Mother," the little girl replies and sits down next to a blond youth.

Subsequently, five others give the same reply: Vera, Pavel, Petr, Nadezhda and Mariia.

Two elderly people in the front dock keep silent and their sharp eyes gleam with hatred.

"I am suffering for my faith," the woman says finally.

L. V. Mikriukova had ten children. But her family did not know any laughter, no gay children playing interrupted the dull silence. *From early in the morning till late at night, religious psalms were sung in the room, books smelling with rot and incense were read.* Children, shivering from fear, would hide under the bed.

The little things grew in the Mikriukov family, deprived of joy, happiness or light. They missed school activities, avoided other children of their age and never attended movies.

"As long as I live, you are not going to belong to the Pioneers," the mother shouted when she saw the red scarves on Vera's and Liuba's necks. Blows followed and the red calico was torn to shreds.

So it went on until Mrs. Mikriukov's son from the first marriage, Robert Malozemov, a *Komsomol* member, came home from the Army. The mother planned to make him a "preacher of the word of God." But she was not successful. School, *Komsomol*, the Army, his factory ... made him look at the Baptist fanaticism of his mother with different eyes.

With Robert's appearance, happy changes came into the family. The children were attracted by the happy, full-of-life *Komsomol* boy. Radio was heard in the house. The stepfather broke the wiring three times, but each time Robert patiently fixed it. He would take the children to the puppet theater and to the circus or on a trip out of town, and he brought them interesting books from the library. In the spring he bought them a T.V. set.

"I am going to throw this devil's machine out of the window," the stepfather threatened.

And the mother shouted:

"You are not my children any more. God will punish you. I am not going to feed and clothe you!"

"We'll manage ourselves," Robert replied quietly.

Six children were now in his arms. He was with them all day long: it was necessary to prepare the meals, to feed the youngest, to mend their clothing, to help children in their homework. And in the evening he went to the factory to work the night shift. It was good that his fellow workers at the Communist Labor Shop, where Robert is employed, are with him. They are helping their friend.

Now, the People's Court of the Moscow Region hears the case concerning the guardianship of the six children of L. V. and D. V. Mikriukov.

"I request that the Court places the children in my care for upbringing. They should be removed from the black net of the Baptists and brought up to be true Soviet people. I am a *Komsomol* member and am responsible for my brothers and sisters. We will manage; we have many friends. The three youngest are still with the parents. They should not be left there to be harmed. . . ."

The People's Court decided to place six children of the Mikriukovs in the care of Robert Malozemov for upbringing. Until the children come of age, alimony will be taken from their parents.

Leningrad, June 8th (by phone)
V. Averin,
Our correspondent

Source: *Sovetskaia Moldaviia*, Kishinev, August 23, 1963

18

The Trial Should Be Continued

The defendant did not hide anything; he answered all questions in detail.

"Where did the Jehovist literature come from which you distributed?" the presiding Judge asked.

"From across the ocean."

"Did it have anti-Soviet character?"

"Yes."

"Do you admit that your activity was criminal?"

"Not only do I admit it; I condemn it and I am breaking

with the Underground for ever. I regret that I lost my young years, that I lived eighteen years for nothing. . . ."

Hundreds of people who filled the hall of the Cultural Center of Rascani were listening with tense attentiveness to every word of the defendant. On the faces of the members of the sect there were guarded looks and confusion; in the eyes of some "sisters" and "brothers" there are sparkles of hate. What is happening to Zaporojan? He seems transformed.

Ivan Zaporojan was known as an ardent member of the organization "Jehovah's Witnesses," not only by the sectarians of the village of Vasileutsi but also by those of other villages. *In 1945 he joined the "Heralds of Eternal Kingdom" and, with all his soul, attached himself to Jehovah's religious teaching. A year later he was condemned for refusing to serve in the Soviet Army.* He returned home in 1949, and again engaged in the same activities as before. *In 1950 another draft notice came from the regional drafting board and Zaporojan repeated the same thing for which he had served his term before. "I am not going to the Army," he said, "my religion does not permit us to take arms in our hands." The "servant of God" was sentenced with all severity of Law for desertion and anti-Soviet propaganda.*

To the Soviet State, man is more valuable than anything else. Therefore, its Laws are so humane, and therefore, Ivan Zaporojan was set free before his term had expired. They thought that this man had thought over his situation and had thrown out of his mind and heart everything that connected him with the shameful past. He would live a new life and start thinking the right way. *Yet having returned to Vasileutsi in 1956, he again went to see the sectarian leaders.*

"I appoint you to be the servant of the circle and a liaison," P. Geletiuk, the area manager at that time, told him.

Three years passed, and Zaporojan became deputy servant of the group. *From Geletiuk he received the journal* Bashnia Strazhi [*Watchtower*] *and other secret publications and distributed them among the sectarians, then delivered coded accounts to the "Area servant."*

It was not with good purposes that the sectarians assembled in Zaporojan's house at night. They befouled with dirt our reality and prayed for the advent of Armageddon.

"Do not vote in the elections, do not join the Soviet

Army, do not get active in public affairs, because God does not like it," he taught the rank-and-file sectarians.

Zaporojan used every opportunity to make people come to him: their need of support, their failures or their weaknesses . . .

Well, what happened to Zaporojan? Why did the active preacher of Jehovism make a complete about face and turn his back on the Underground? Why doesn't he, as before, defend the organization of the "Jehovah's Witnesses" but, on the contrary, unmasks it? Has the leader shrunk in the face of punishment?

Ivan Zaporojan wrote his declaration about his break with the Jehovists on June 8, 1963, soon after his arrest. But it was not dictated by the feeling of fear. After all, he was tried before and he was not afraid, because he deeply believed. Now, however, this belief was not present any more, but, instead, there was realization of the senselessness of further work underground. . . .

It was the thought that the organization of "Jehovah's Witnesses" suffers bankruptcy in the Soviet country, that it was time to end the double life, that penetrated Zaporojan's conscience four years ago. He tried to chase this thought away from his mind, he regarded it as Satan's delusion, but he was not able to get rid of this realization.

Before his eyes, the sect dispersed; it was deserted not only by some rank-and-file believers, but also by some leaders, such as the area manager Pavel Geletiuk, the section servant Petr Syrgi. . . . Also depressing was the break between the leaders of Jehovism in Siberia, which, as Zaporojan learned, was caused by their disagreement concerning the division money. It appeared that there, at the top, people believed not in God but in their worldly life.

Slowly, the enlightenment came about and it was only the sentiment of strict Jehovist discipline developed over many years, and also *his wife, blinded by fanaticism, who would not even hear of any break with "brothers" and "sisters," that kept him on the old road. So, when Zaporojan was arrested, he finally could breathe freely*. Time had come to put a dot over the past. At the investigation, he admitted everything honestly, told in detail about his improper activities and wrote the declaration concerning his break with the antisocial organization of the Jehovah's Witnesses.

Eighteen years he lived in vain. . . . Ivan Zaporojan had

to pay a high price for his enlightenment. The presiding Judge, I. A. Guranda, more than once mentioned these eighteen lost years to the sectarians present in the courtroom. He wanted these people, who had not yet freed themselves from the influence of religious ideology, to learn a lesson from the bitter experience of Zaporojan and to realize that they not only deprive themselves of the joys of a vigorous, creative and inspired life but, also willingly or unwillingly, take part in an antisocial activity of the organization Jehovah's Witnesses and in its criminal connections with the American imperialism.

The workers of the Rascani District, present in the courtroom, amply learned how pitiful was the role of the rank-and-file faithfuls who became victims of Jehovism.

Although the presiding Judge ordered several short recesses, the trial essentially did not stop for even a minute. As soon as the Judges left their seats and the guards removed the defendant, the *kolkhoz* members, workers and educated people would surround the sectarians and start a really heated conversation with them. Some appealed to the human pride of the erring ones, others talked about the absurdities of which the Bible is full, still others put them to shame and pointed out the harmfulness of "Jehovah's Witnesses". . . . And the *"heralds of Kingdom" (mostly women) said something about God and Armageddon* (the place where, according to the book of Revelation, the last battle of history will take place).

These oral skirmishes involuntarily brought to our minds the thought: *Why is it so seldom that such community trials take place against the sectarianism in our villages, settlements, towns—where there still remain those "witnesses" and other "brothers" and "sisters" in Christ? Aren't we too yielding to people who speculate with the belief in God? Why do we sometimes miss the realization of our right to an active, continuous and militant antireligious propaganda?*

The present Court trial showed that *the atheists from Vasileutsi attack the obsolete vestiges rather timidly and do not make war on the criminal Jehovist propaganda.* Five of six comrades who appeared as witnesses called themselves agitators. But not a single one of them answered [in the positive] to the question of the judges: "With whom of the believers do you work? Whom did you get out of the sect?"

The sectarian Vera Zabolotna is even a relative of the

agitator Maria Tsymbaliuk. When the presiding Judge, Ivan Afanasievich Guranda, asked Maria whether she talked to Vera about her erring, there was a reply:

"*I did not,* she lives outside of my section. . . ."

Also the other agitators, whom we had the opportunity to hear at that trial, "work" the same way with the believers. They met the sectarians only in *selsovet*—the village council, when the Jehovah's Witnesses were summoned there to explain whether they would participate in the elections of the organs of administration.

The candid admission of the defendant as to his mistakes and his condemnation of his harmful underground activity were appreciated by the Court; Zaporojan was sentenced conditionally to ten years in prison with a three-year term of probation.

The testimony of thirteen witnesses and the convincing, well-founded statements of the public prosecutor—the headmaster of the school at Nagoriansk, V. K. Kasianenko, and of the State Prosecutor, A. P. Poluiektov, will surely leave their impact on the consciousness of the rank-and-file sectarians, and will help them to realize that *the adherence to this reactionary organization constitutes a crime against the country and the people.*

The trial which ended in Rascani should be continued in Vasileutsi and other villages. Let our atheists be judges at these trials of conscience! Every day a fight should start for a new man. Massively, actively and persuasively one should expose all and sundry religious survivals, and help those who still have the bad luck of being under the influence of a religious ideology, including the Jehovist one, to return to a healthy and valuable life.

Settlement of Rascani
N. Chernous,
Our special correspondent

Source: *Pravda Vostoka* (Truth of the East), November 15, 1963

19

Such Things Are Not Forgiven

From the Courtroom:

The assizes of the District Court of Andizhan [Uzbekistan, U.S.S.R., Translator] at a public trial in Namangan considered the criminal case of illegal meetings of a non-registered Baptist sect.

In the dock, there were ardent preachers of baptism, Maria Shevchuk, Taisiia Tkachenko, Ekaterina Vekazina.

For three days the Court thoroughly investigated the matter, heard the testimony of the accused and of witnesses. This made it possible to establish the criminal activities of the accused.

Maria Shevchuk has a daughter, a son-in-law and grandchildren. The State provided her with a pension. She could live and enjoy life. *Yet this uneducated, fanatical woman became one of the organizers of the secret Baptist sect at Namangan, and a leader at secret meetings of the sect. People often talked to her and explained that her "activities" were harmful to society. Nothing helped.*

She maintained:

"I became a Baptist because God had placed me in the society. He cured me from a serious illness."

"Did you turn to physicians, too, at that time?" the Judge asked.

"Yes, I turned to the physicians, too"—and she added hastily—"but, obviously, God cures the sick ones through people." Then she continued: "I started seeking those who believed. Sometimes we would visit some sick woman and pray to God that He might save her."

"Well, did He save them?"

"He did."

"And did you call a physician?"

"We did," Mrs. Shevchuk mumbled to a general laughter of those present in the courtroom.

Mrs. Shevchuk attempted to lure into the nets of the

sect Mrs. E. F. Karpova, her seriously sick brother, Iuri Karpov and some others, but met with their rebuttal

The fanatical woman managed to control the life of her granddaughter Liuba. *Mrs. Shevchuk made her copy songs and verses from Old Testament books published in Tsarist Russia, and distribute the texts of the so-called Baptist Hymn.* It is easy to imagine how all this affected the girl and the formation of her character and philosophy of life.

Shevchuk succeeded in getting into the sect Taisiia Tkachenko and Ekaterina Vekazina. They became equally fanatical in all their behavior and activities, and affected adversely those around them.

The accused Tkachenko, among other things, said:

"One night I heard a divine song from Heaven and wrote it down."

But this "sister in Christ" was caught lying. She was shown at the Court an old book from which she copied the "divine song from Heaven." Yet many had believed her.

Working at a clothes factory, Taisiia Tkachenko told the women workers:

"You are walking on the wrong pathway, you are lost sheep."

This meant: life in this world is vanity of vanities and, therefore, one should wait for a paradise of life in heaven.

Ekaterina Vekazina, like her "sisters," propagated baptism and organized meetings. When asked by the Judge what was the purpose of inducing people to the sect, she lied, dodged and, finally, admitted:

"We wanted to make all people join."

Along with the "sisters in Christ," there sat in the dock Georgii Vekazin, a juvenile, but ostensibly a spoiled youth. This year, in February, he returned from a labor colony where he served his time for theft. He did not want to work or study, but, encouraged by his fanatical mother, he led a parasitic way of life. He made a "friendship" with a fourteen-year-old girl who lived in the neighborhood. The neighbors often drew the attention of the parents to the obviously abnormal development of this "friendship." Yet nobody would take any precautions: "God would settle everything." And so, while the parents prayed, Georgii, using physical strength and threatening with death, raped the girl.

In her last word, the accused Tkachenko said among other things:

"We are not liked in Namagan."

This is true. Well, and why, we could ask, should people like Mrs. Tkachenko, Mrs. Shevchuk and the Vekazins? Because they tried to divert people from our vigorous life, from the participation in the structure of Communism? Because they tried to make people believe in "life in paradise after death"? Or, perhaps, because they crippled the lives of children? No, nobody can like this and these things are not forgiven!

The Court, in the name of the people, sentenced M. N. Shevchuk, T. D. Tkachenko and E. K. Vekazina to two years in prison each, and Georgii Vekazin—to eight years in prison.

Kh. Kirgizbeeva,
City Attorney

I. Malenkov,
Correspondent of *Pravda Vostoka,*
         not of the staff

Source: *Sovetskaia Rossiia,* December 22, 1963

20

Scales Fell from the Eyes

From the Courtroom:

"Do they justly try your son?" the Judge asks.

Deadly silence fell upon the courtroom. One minute of silence seemed very long. All were awaiting what the elderly, graying man had to say. After all, his own son was there, in the dock. The Court procedure had only started, no sentence had been passed yet and he, the father, was to be the first judge. It is not easy, but he says:

"Yes, they are right to try him. He is guilty."

Now what was it that Ian Pinka had done? Why does he sit as a defendant in the dock?

... Once upon a time, there appeared on the streets of Klaipeda a young, slim man. His arrival was not noticed. The people who passed by him could not guess that they saw the very "Messenger of a living God." But this was what he announced during the next meeting of the sect of the Pentecostals.

"I have come to you from God Himself, in order to save those who are deep in sins."

No matter how submissive the flock was, how intensively the leaders tried to bluff them, the people could not seriously believe that the "Messenger of God" fell down to them from heaven. Where did he live before? But this was a matter which the "God's" man was least inclined to discuss. After all, he had spent the past five years in prison, serving his time for robbery.

"I suffered for my faith in God," Pinka lied without even blinking his eye. "I was in prison . . . for the truth. . . ."

He looked sternly and imperatively into the eyes of his flock; the sectarians could not bear his gaze and looked down humbly, submissively.

Having thus frightened the sectarians, Pinka did whatever he pleased. He made the sectarians fast and take nothing into their mouths for three to four days, but he himself misappropriated their money and lived to his heart's delight. He forbade the faithful to attend movies, to read newspapers or to turn to physicians for medical help, but he himself went to seaside resorts to rest.

During the praying sessions, he would bring people to hysterics and loss of consciousness while he was quietly watching how they tortured themselves.

A young woman, a resident of Klaipeda, Titepe, was separated from her husband and temporarily in a difficult situation. Taking advantage of this, the fanatics dragged her into their sect. She was to pay a high price for her trust.

The woman became seriously ill. Her temperature would rise rapidly and she often lost her consciousness.

"It is for your sins that God sent this suffering upon you," Pinka blasphemed. "Get up and pray!" he ordered her.

Only the interference of the neighbors, who called for an ambulance, saved the life of the woman.

A member of the sect, one "sister" Anna, fell seriously ill as a result of exhausting prayers and fasting. In a half-insane state of mind, she believed she had heard "the voice of God" which promised to lift her up to the third heaven. In order to better fly to the address indicated, she sold up all her movables. At present she is under treatment in a mental hospital.

It was revealed in the course of the trial that the sectarians were preparing their own trial against "sister" Malysheva. During a prayer session, the "voice from Heaven" ordered that her fingers and her head were to be cut off. It should be said that choosing her was not accidental. Malysheva had many doubts and, worst of all, she wore a modern hairdo, was manicured and attended movies, by which she lead other "sisters" into temptation. This is the reason why they were preparing to try her. However, Malysheva escaped from the prayers and never came again.

In 1961 Pinka moved to the Smolensk Region. Here, too, he would not abandon his criminal occupation. He was warned several times, but nothing helped.

. . . The trial is over. Now everybody understands why even his own father had said:

"Yes, they are right to try him. He is guilty."

Ian Pinka was sentenced to five years in prison.

N. Iakovlev

1964

Source: *Uchitelskaia Gazeta* (Teacher's Gazette), January 18, 1964

21

Sectarians on Trial

Riga (T.A.S.S. correspondence). Hundreds of toiling people of the village crowded in the auditorium of the Community House in the town of Viesite. Here the assizes of the People's Court of the Ekabpilskii Region was in session, trying the case against the Pentecostals—sectarians, Ianis and Zenta Osma. Before the Court there appeared as witnesses—the director of the Secondary School of Viesite, V. Polisktov, the supervisor of the teaching department of this school, A. Lapinia, the teacher, Mrs. Ia. Kivlenieste, the "Brigadier" of the Sel-Khos cooperative "Viesite," A. Dabolin, and others. They testified that *the married couple Osma, every Sunday make their children attend prayers where the sectarians, in a state of religious fanaticism, sing earsplitting songs.* The children are forbidden to read fine literature, attend movie theaters, school gatherings, concerts or watch television programs. No wonder that Ruta, Ianis and Peteris are poor students, behave antisocially and are physically and mentally poorly developed.

"I am exchanging children for God," Ianis Osma admitted frankly.

The Community Prosecutors proposed that the sectarians be stripped of their parental rights and their children be given to the State for upbringing.

The People's Court sustained this motion. Ianis and Zenta Osma, who seriously violated Soviet Laws concerning the bringing up of the young generation, were deprived of parental power.

Source. *Kazakhstanskaia Pravda*, February 8, 1964

22

According to their Merits

From the Courtroom:

"I.P.K.H.S."—this is the abbreviation of the name of a sect of obscurantists (Union of True Orthodox Christians), whose dark deeds were described in *Kazakhstanskaia Pravda* of December 8, 1963.

For a few days, a trial against the leaders of the sect was conducted at Alma Ata. One after another the witnesses appeared and an obscure picture of the doings in the Underground of the "I.P.K.H.S." was revealed in its full nakedness. In especially prepared hiding places, the sectarians would indulge in fasting and prayers.

Margarita Tortsova spent nearly seven years in the *Underground*. Appearing before the Court, she stated:

"I am grateful to the people who helped me to escape from the realm of darkness and obscurantism. Now, for a few months I have been working at the Novokuznetsk metal factory as an electro-solderer. I was qualified as fourth class."

Now the sentence was passed.

For anti-Soviet propaganda and agitation, for production, storage and distribution of literature of libelous contents, for leadership in an Underground sect, the activity of which, conducted in the form of the execution of religious practices, was combined with causing harm to health and with infringement upon the rights of citizens, Aleksiej Grigorovich Bogatyrev, alias Mina Mikhajlovich Serafimov, alias Aleksiej Grigorievich Lablonskii, alias Mina, the Monk, was sentenced to seven years in prison with confinement in a colony of correctional labor with a strict regime.

Grigorii Perevishin, alias Vasilii Nikolaevich, alias Varlaam, the Monk, was sentenced to five years in prison with confinement in a colony of correctional labor with a strict regime.

For active participation in anti-Soviet activities of the

Underground sect, for preparation of hideouts in his home where, with his knowledge, slanderous anti-Soviet literature was stored, for giving his house for the carrying out of sectarian meetings, Viktor Vasilevich Karlin was sentenced to three years in prison with confinement in a colony of correctional labor with a strict regime.

Those present at the trial heard the sentence with unanimous approval.

Source: *Pravda Vostoka* (Truth of the East), February 29, 1964

23

Fanaticism of the Believers and Indifference of the Atheists

The public trial of a group of more active members of the illegal community of the Evangelical Christian Baptists was approaching its conclusion, when there appeared in the club hall of the kcnaf plant, an employee of the Tashkent art factory. Watching the dock and noticing Aleksei Neverov in it, she was greatly surprised. Lenia Neverov? It couldn't be. But he was a handsome boy, a conscientious worker!

I heard many similar statements during that trial. Not only in respect to Neverov but also in respect to his fellow defendants in the dock, Boris Garmashov and Aksen Zubov, the latter, by the way, being Aleksei Neverov's father-in-law.

Well, how did it happen that these people, so different from each other but, at the same time somehow strikingly resembling each other, found themselves before the Court? Could it be an accident, some kind of fatal mistake? Not at all, everything was in order.

But let us start at the beginning and get acquainted with them more closely!

Here is Aleksei Neverov. A strong, healthy man, thirty years of age. Father of five. Learned master in textile design in the art factory. A precise, conscientious worker, a little nervous, but, in general, a polite man—this is how his fellow workers and neighbors described him. True, in the characteristics of Neverov, supplied by the factory and attached to his (naturally, criminal) case, we can read the following words: "He lost the feeling of collectiveness, he shuns the collective."

"He lost the feeling of collectiveness." These bitter words well explain the core of the matter. All his life as an intelligent being, Neverov has been under an influence which is strange to our system and to our society. This is his tragedy.

Still as a student at the art college and as a *Komsomol*, Aleksei was not so eager to learn but rather to have an easy life. During his free time, together with his older brother, Vladimir, also a student, he learned another "lesson," a "lesson" in robbing and stealing. The effect was quite logical. In 1952 the two bad brothers were caught at one "job" and wound up behind bars; Vladimir received eighteen years and Aleksei fifteen years in prison. But Aleksei served less than one-third of the penalty. In 1955 he was freed by an amnesty.

It would seem that the severe punishment would bring Aleksei to his senses, make him think over his way of life and decide to straighten it out. But nothing like that happened. Another obstacle appeared in his way. This time it was an obstacle in the form of religious opiate. Neverov did not have the strength to overcome it and found himself in the community of Evangelical Christian Baptists.

But this alone was not too bad. The Constitution of our country guarantees freedom of conscience. Religious beliefs are a private matter of every Soviet citizen. Our government guarantees the right freely to perform religious rites, and does not interfere in the activities of religious associations. On the other hand, religious organizations and groups have no right to interfere in government matters. In other words, *the freedom of practicing religious rites is guaranteed only to the extent to which it does not violate public order* and is not connected with infringement of the rights of the citizens of the U.S.S.R. And it should be said that the great majority of the believers strictly observe these laws. But not all of them. To some of them, these laws are like bones stuck in their throats. Aleksei Neverov, as it happened, found himself in this category, along with Boris Garmashov and Aksen Zubov.

Boris Garmashov's outer appearance is pleasant. Handsome, built like an athlete, a young man. "He should rather play soccer than read sermons," someone in the courtroom noted. He is married, has two children and his wife is expecting a third one. His education—ten grades [primary school]. His profession—stove inspector. He worked in the building department of *Tashoblpotrebsoiuz* [name of the Tashkent Provincial enterprise].

Early in his youth Boris lost his father. His mother, a very little-educated, highly religious woman, gave him a "corresponding" education. Boris, as they say, *with his mother's milk received the religious opiate which, step by step, poisoned his mind.*

And, finally, there is *Aksen Flegontovich Zubov, an elderly man grown wise with life's experience. In his defense speech, he told, not without pride, that he worked for a quarter of a century as a locksmith at the first shoe factory, had many privileges and more than once received a bonus for good work.*

A few years ago, Zubov retired. But the quiet life was a burden to him. So he *became utterly absorbed in the antisocial activities of the illegal community of the Baptists.*

How did the antisocial work of Neverov, Garmashov and Zubov show? They knowingly opposed the existing laws which regulated the performance of religious cults. *Without official permission of the authorities, they organized at Kuiluk an illegal community and systematically met for secret prayers in the home of one H. Matiukhina as well as in the apartments of other believers.*

In 1961, under the direction of the illegal organizing committee created near Moscow by such archparasites and charlatans as G. Kriuchenko and A. Prokofiev (*Pravda Vostoka* wrote about the latter in October 1962), *Neverov and Garmashov organized the so-called initiative group and started a vigorous provocative activity among the believers, instigating them in the disobedience to the Soviet Laws. They maliciously libeled our system, demanded full freedom of action for themselves, i.e. freedom to conduct religious propaganda, which means freedom of coercion of human conscience.*

Neverov, Garmashov and Zubov frequently received in their homes Prokofiev, Kriuchenko, Zakharov and other noted Underground missionaries and obediently placed at their disposal the tribunes for reactionary sermons. They would copy and distribute among the believers provocative literature (domestic and foreign), various papers, announcements, appeals and protests. As if this was not enough, they arranged, individually or in groups, listening sessions of special sermons broadcast in the Russian language by the radio transmitters from the U.S.A., Canada and Ecuador, recorded them on tapes and then distributed them in various ways.

Naturally, they, as well as their "ideological leaders" clearly see and hear that the masses of the Soviet people are not only indifferent to religion but totally reject it. In this respect, the admission contained in the handwritten, anonymous booklet: *God or Nature*, is very characteristic. Here it is: "At our age of crude materialism, the rejection of God became fashionable. Atheism deeply penetrated the minds not only of people of low education but also those of so-called high education who, using their diplomas, pretend to know absolute truth which, as they maintain, they have found in the materialism."

This is why Neverov, Garmashov and Zubov, their advisers and leaders, put special stress in their activities on withdrawing unstable young people from social life and on leading them into the world of mysticism and superstition. They used as a directive in this activity the article, in part anonymous, "The enemies of the Christian youth."

What is it that the authors of that article declare to be enemies of the youth? First of all "bad books" which include all literature except the Bible. They explain: The reading of "bad books" leads to a cooling-off attitude to the Bible and to the "divine work." In the subsequent chapters the authors warn the "Christian" youth against uniting with nonbelieving people within their age group, call upon the youth not to attend theaters and movies, not to go to parks, not to participate in mass cultural plays and sports competition, qualifying all this as a "mirage" and "devil's bait." In conclusion, there is a man-hating statement: "Friendship with the world means hostility to God."

Well, and what is it that they propose to fill the leisure

time of the young people with? In this case, their program is not very extensive: Pray zealously, study the Bible and you will "achieve spiritual salvation and balance." Well, is it not rather little? Now in order to somehow attract the youth to the "divine work," our "heroes" organized out-of-town excursions, children and youth meetings, all kinds of circles of artistic activities, and "evenings of love." Such circles and "evenings" were arranged in the premises of Zubov and Garmashov and in other places. But, again, all these means would come to one thing: study of the Bible, recitals of religious verses and singing of religious songs. Poisoned by religious opiates, Neverov and Garmashov also attempt to poison the minds of their children, compel them to pray to God, to learn poems and songs assigned to them, and forbid them to play with neighbors' children. They severely punish their children for every disobedience.

It is difficult to tell, in detail, about all the criminal activities of Neverov, Garmashov and Zubov, to judge to the full extent and to evaluate the moral harm which they afflicted on themselves and the people around them. The damage they caused is great. Yet, we wish to dwell longer on one particular aspect of their activities.

In their sermons they openly called upon the believing young people to use religious reasons to avoid service in the Soviet Army, and, should this prove impossible, they urge them not to carry arms. Furthermore, their action was not limited to the sermons. In his correspondence with his younger brother, Sergei, who served in the Navy, Neverov tried to incite him to refuse to carry arms and instructed him how to make religious propaganda among the sailors. But what has religion to do with it? Nothing at all. This is all politics and, at that, anti-Soviet politics.

Could the Soviet Government tolerate such politics and such activities? Naturally—no. So, the criminals received just punishment.

With this, we could put the period and end the story. But there is more to talk about and to think about. Naturally, it is right that the criminal fanatics be separated from the society. But here they live and work among us, their like-minded fellows and "Brothers-in-arms." Many of them are sincere in their delusion but are under the influence of people who are not, as a rule, concerned about their fate. One would like to hope that the last trial would make them stop and think about the sense and objectives of their lives and activities, and would open their eyes and make them see that there is only one step from the malicious fanaticism to a crime against the State. The example of Neverov, Garmashov and Zubov is ample evidence of this truth.

And, a second thing. The Court trial against Neverov, Garmashov and Zubov exposed serious shortcomings in the ideological and educational work of some lower level party organizations; their lack of attention and indifference to the spiritual world of people. After all, it is true that the religious influence penetrates where there is no systematic, interesting and manifold in its form, educational work and a tactful, individual approach to human beings. And, the other way around, where people are always in plain view, and where they feel the attention directed at them, the religious survivals vanish.

In this respect, the story of Eduard Nakhtigal is very instructive. From his early years, Edik (diminutive from Eduard) was brought up in a religious spirit and then became an ardent Baptist. Then, in 1959, he was drafted and called to serve in the ranks of the Soviet Army. When he was ready to go for induction, the most important thing among the treasures of the inductee was, probably, the Bible. Now, the service went under way. At the beginning, Nakhtigal shunned his comrades, refused to carry arms and stubbornly studied the "divine" book.

The commanding officers of the unit and his fellow soldiers were able to find a key to the heart of the young man and to conquer the religious opiate. So, Nakhtigal threw the Bible into, pardon me, the latrine, joined the ranks of V.L.K.S.M. and became an exemplary soldier.

However, after the demobilization, Nakhtigal stumbled again. His parents and an old friend succeeded in converting the "prodigal son" to the old faith. Obviously, here we have a man who quite easily trades his principles and is not able to form his own firm convictions. Greatly responsible for this state of affairs are his fellow workers at the Technological Rubber Articles Factory where Nakhtigal is presently employed.

It is no secret that we still have many party and government leaders who tend to judge a man merely according to his productive value. If a worker performs his norm at the rate of 105 to 110 per cent, if he is not loafing, then everything is all right. And what he does after work, how he lives, how he brings up his children—this is his private affair. And only when such a man appears at the edge of an abyss, they naïvely ask themselves: "How could it have happened?" It is exactly the way the employee of the art factory was surprised when she saw Neverov in the dock.

In order to prevent this, it is necessary to remove the shortcoming in our ideological work and come closer to people and their lives. A militant and purposeful work in the field of atheistic education constitutes an important segment of the ideological front. No Communist, regardless of the position he holds, can and has the right to evade this issue.

V. Ziuganov

Source: *Komsomolskaia Pravda*, April 10, 1964

24

A Proud Badge

(Reason against religion)

Every morning a long line of trucks leaves, through the gate, the premises of the Automobile Pool Management of Kremerovo.

I well know the truck No. WH I 44-46 and its driver. His name is Maerov. Aleksandr Maerov. I met him three years ago. He is a Siberian, a young man of twenty-six. When I see him at the driving wheel I can hardly believe that, only a short time ago, his name was Father Aleksandr. . . .

The little village of Sergeevka is located far away from a town and from the railroad. With its log cabins and fences made of planks, it virtually nestles in the *taiga* (vast Siberian forest) and hides under huge cedars and firs. Kiril Longinovich Maerov liked Sergeevka and, late in the twenties, he moved here, escaping collectivization. *"I do not want to work together with the Antichrists,"* said he.

Long hours would he kneel in front of the icons, bow to the cold boards of the floor, and pray to God for His grace. Seven children followed their father's example. Continually, he impressed upon the children that people are merely guests on earth and, in order to get into the Paradise, one should not offend God.

Sasha (diminutive from Aleksandr) had difficulties in his studies. For one year, he did not attend school at all and two winters he spent in the fifth grade. For this his church was responsible. *Nobody in the school knew that in the evenings Sasha had to burn the incense for the church, put the candles in place and take care of the articles of the church service.*

Sasha finished his *semiletka* (seven years' basic school) when he was eighteen. What should he do next? Study? Work? But the father decided:

"Go to the seminary."

It was within the walls of the seminary that the first doubts as to the truth of religion came to Sasha's mind. He was afraid to talk about it openly: after all, *the seminarians were taught that all doubts in the existence of God come "from the devil," and that they were supposed simply to believe in everything that was written in the holy books. Also, there was no time for deep thoughts. From early morning to late at night they had to learn by heart psalms and other verses as well as evangelical and biblical texts.*

Once, Sasha mentioned his doubts to his fellow seminarian. The latter replied: "Don't think of nonsense, what do you need it for? You should think of the way to get a rich parish."

The inconsistencies of the religious teaching, and the surrounding atmosphere of love of money and a safe and comfortable life brought about Sasha's disappointment. *He started to pray even more.* Yet his doubts did not disappear. Then, *the idea came to his mind that only by serving the church would he be delivered from his tribulations, and that only by becoming a minister and devoting himself entirely to the service of God would he find the truth.*

Before becoming a minister, Maerov was supposed to get married. Meeting his father, Aleksandr mentioned marriage. Kiril Longinovich asked:

"And who is the bride? Is she baptized?"

It was evident that his son's selection did not please him: "Zina Malyshenko, an orphan who grew up in a modest and poor family."

Seeing that his son was stubborn, the father tried a cunning trick: He prepared five slips with the names of five girls he picked, placed the slips into the gospel, put the book for the night under the icon in the corner and prayed for a long time. In the morning he gave his son the slip with the name of his future wife, alledgedly chosen by God himself.

Sasha was not to be shaken in his decision and opposed the will of his father.

Exactly at the age of twenty, Sasha became a deacon and after three more months, a priest in the parish of Shunga, some seven kilometers from Kostroma.

Long hours and days passed in meditation on the sense of life. The temptation would come to him to engage in a real life and to take a job, any job, if only it would be useful to society. Sasha envied the people who hurried to work in the morning, envied boisterous boys and girls who climbed the trucks with their spades and pails and went to the fields.

He knew that his abandoning the priesthood would be met with "bayonets fixed" [sic]. But that was not what scared him. He was much more concerned with the question as to whether he would be able to find his place in life.

So, Aleksandr wrote a report to the eparchial office at Kostroma:

"After a long-lasting meditation and analysis of the religious dogmas I came to the firm conclusion that I had not chosen the right course in my life, because I found the whole inconsistency of the religious teaching. I cannot preach what I do not now firmly believe. Therefore, I took a firm decision to break with the religion, to take off my pastoral garb and take up a job useful for the community. I took the liberty to take this step conscientiously and firmly."

Avraam, the superior monk, came to Shunga for negotiations.

"Do not sin before God, Father Aleksandr! If two and a half thousand rubles are not enough, we double this amount. You are young and we are going to create a paradise on earth for you. . . ." the messenger of the bishop persuaded.

But Maerov would not yield. This made the monk mad and he started threatening:

"You traitor to Christ! You will die from starvation! You don't know how to do anything!"

Aleksandr could not remain at Shunga any longer.

In the summer of 1960 Sasha came to Kremerovo. His father would not believe that his son had taken off the priest's cross and garb for ever. He still hoped to see Sasha in charge of his parish in the Znamenskoi church. When he saw that his son had finally broken with religion, he said with malice: *"You crucified Christ!* You are going to wallow like a dog under a fence! There is no room for you in my house any more!"

Sasha went out to look for a job in factories and construction enterprises. No sense in denying: he had to swallow many a bitter pill. Some would say: "No openings. We do not need students." Others advised him to come and inquire again in a week or two. Still others ... Take, for example, the automobile repair factory at Kremerovo. Sasha even filed an application: he decided to learn to become a tinsmith. But here was the trouble: he could not produce his work book, because Maerov did not have one. The Chief of the Department of Manpower sternly asked:

"Have you come out of prison?"

"No, from Kostroma. . . "

"Well, what happened, did you stay with your parents on their support until you became twenty-three?"

"I was an employee of a cult association."

"Well, then, you better take your application and get lost. Stay away from sins!"

Once, Sasha visited the editor's office of the paper *Komsomolets Kuzbasa*. He was received there sincerely, like a friend. Having heard his story, they called up Comrade Mironov, Deputy Chief of the managing committee of *Proftekhobrazovanie* [professional technical training].

On the same day, Aleksandr was enrolled in the Third Technical School.

Sasha's scholastic achievements were no worse than those of others. True, he did not have the scholarship. For six months he worked at night as an automobile mechanic and driver at the Predzavodskaia Automobile Base. They celebrated an open house in a new apartment: the Town

Executive Committee did not neglect the Maerov family in its need.

Recently, Sasha passed his entrance examination to a higher school. He was transferred to the Fourth Automobile Pool Management. The managers accepted him into their family without unnecessary inquiries, without any reproaches for his past. He works like all others—and is writing his "work biography."

But Sasha does not break his relations with Kostroma. He corresponds with *Komsomol* members and Pioneers and advises parents to keep children away from the churchmen. Sasha's letters are full of joy and optimism.

"Each of us has his own feast days. They are something special, remembered all your life. For me, such a feast was the day when I joined the *Komsomol*. The members of my age had received their red badges at the age of fifteen; I received it at the age of twenty-six."

I remember how in the fall of 1958, I came to the Regional committee of *Komsomol*. I had studied the "law," assuming that they would examine me. Instead, they asked me to tell them my story. There were so many young people gathered in the room that there were no seats or even standing room left. They applauded. . . . They shook my hands. . . . They approved, were happy for me.

From there, directly from the meeting, I went to the corn harvest. And when I came back, they handed me in the *Komsomol* card. I pinned the badge to the lapel of my jacket, hung the jacket on the back of a chair. . . . It was such a bright badge, with Lenin's silhouette on it . . . I feel like I have been reborn. On my chest, there is now not a cross, but a proud badge of V.L.K.S.M. [All-Union League of Communist Youth]. I realize that the membership in *Komsomol* places on me many obligations. I promise to work and live in a way that would not make me ashamed to look into the eyes of the people.

Kremerovo
M. Shcherbakov

Source: *Sovetskaia Justitsia* (Soviet Justice) No. 9, May 1964

25

With the Cross on their Chests and with Switches in their Hands

On a dark night, when the deadly silence was only interrupted from time to time by the occasional barkings of a sleepy dog, small windows in a little slate-covered wooden house were dimly lighted for the brethren in Christ. Sneaking, scared of their own shadows, there came people from all sides. The servants of God with amazing agility filled the half-dark room with a low ceiling. With the full assembly of the believers in this room, it became so crowded that it wasn't possible to bow to the floor in reverence to God without hitting one's neighbor's back with the head. Because of the stuffy air, the flame in the lamp was blinking. Streaks of sweat ran down the tired, gloomy faces.

"With all your heart, rest your hope with God and do not rely on your mind," Subbotin the pastor admonished, with his chin up and his eyes with a feverish gleam raised.

In the stinking air, children, not wanting to stay behind the adults, raised up their skinny little arms and then hit the wooden floor with their pale foreheads, asking the Almighty not to be angry with them and to strengthen their weak spirit in faith to Him.

Soon, Subbotin got into a white heat, wildly rolled his eyes, waved his arms and alternately shouted hysterically aloud in a singing voice [*sic*] and turned to a whisper:

"People commit outrages. Having forgotten God, they offend their ears by listening to the radio, they read indecent books, go to the movies and to meetings which divert them from a proper God-pleasing life. . . ."

In the course of a few hours, the tired hearts of the believers were agitated to the utmost by the fiery words of the possessed pastor.

At the same time, outside on the street, hiding in a corner stood guard one of "God's servants," guarding the meeting against the ever-present workers and representatives of the government and also against a possible unwanted invasion by any blasphemous intruder.

. . .

Liubov Mikhailovna Khmara took the pots from the stove, vigorously stirred the cabbage soup with a ladle and poured some into a Thermos bottle. Pleasantly smiling, she looked at the nurse of the local hospital of the Kulundinskii *sovkhoz*, Valentina Mikhailovna Kurganskaia, who came to the kitchen to get food for the sick ones, and in an oily voice, cautiously said:

"Life has become difficult. Even when both husband and wife work in one family, there is always some want of this or that. . . . I really don't know how you can manage all alone with children. . . ."

Not realizing what the cook was hinting at, Valentina Mikhailovna replied in short:

"I do not complain about my fortune."

"You should not force yourself too hard," Liubov Mikhailovna continued, without paying attention to her words. "One should live with people in friendship, then they would help."

"I do not quarrel with anybody and do not offend anybody," the nurse said.

"One should respect good people not forgetting God," Liubov Mikhailovna continued, coming step by step to the point. "And everything will be rewarded to you a hundredfold."

"What hundredfold?" Valentina Mikhailovna got interested.

"They will build you a house and will give you money," Liubov Mikhailovna whispered.

"Who will give it?"

"Brothers." Liubov Mikhailovna disclosed her secret.

"Well, let them give, if they like it," Valentina Mikhailovna smiled.

"Join our sect, recover your belief in God," the cook passionately asked.

"Leave me alone with your sect and your belief," the nurse said angrily. "Give me the Thermos bottle and let me go."

It was not always that the oily voices of the sectarians

succeeded. But this would not bother them too much. They had other ways in their arsenal, by which they sometimes succeeded in scaring people, breaking their will and turning them into believers.

In most cases it was juveniles and children that became their victims. This was the fate, for example, of the eleven-year-old Zuzana Reimer. Her aunt, a Baptist, Elizaveta Petrovna Ul, who worked as a storekeeper in the —— bakery, was enraged by the wish of her niece to become a Pioneer girl, grabbed her arm, pulled her to the cellar and, opening the cover, put the girl into the pit. The girl shouted, cried, banged with her little fists on the wooden cover and called for help. But her voice was lost in the damp underground room without penetrating outside, faded away down there, painfully and hopelessly. Only after a few hours the aunt opened the door and furiously asked her pinched and pale-faced niece:

"Are you going to be a Pioneer girl?"

For Zuzana it was a terrible and frightening experience to stay all alone in the pit, but she would not submit. Ul then applied another terrible measure: she starved her niece. Finally the despotic and cruel aunt succeeded. Zuzana not only refused to join the Pioneer girls but also started attending the meetings of the Baptists.

Also Anatolii Khmara, born in 1951, was to meet God by way of similar methods. Together with his schoolmates, Vitia Lenskii and Vitia Kozrev, he came home one day, happy, shining. His father, Nikolai Kuzmich Khmara, a Baptist, upon seeing a Pioneer scarf around his son's neck, knit his brow in displeasure and called sternly:

"Come here!"

Not knowing about the displeasure boiling in his father's chest and suspecting nothing about his intentions, the son quietly approached him. The father tore off the bright red scarf, cut it to pieces with an axe, gathered the remnants into the palm of his hand to the last shred, threw everything into the fire burning in the stove, made a sign of a cross and sighed, obviously having got rid of an evil spirit.

Soon, he made Tola [Anatolii] and his older son, Vladimir, born in 1950, attend the prayers, learn religious verses and psalms. Now, they pray before and after meals, and read religious verses. At this time, the children are scared to such an extent and deprived of memory that they insist that they left the Pioneers of their own will, that nobody forced them and that they themselves found God.

The brothers have harnessed themselves into the reins of the Baptist faith and are pulling, overtaxing their strength, a burden of the exhausting sectarian rites, beyond the capacity of their age. They have very little time for studying or for sports. There is no wonder that they became poor students.

"How long do the prayers last?"

"No more than four hours," Vladimir explained in his conversation with his teacher.

Four hours—but this is one half of a working day!

The happy childhood is lost for these children, cruelly and mercilessly. Their happiness, their bright laughter and careless play were stolen from them, their childish minds were enmeshed in the web of religious beliefs.

. . .

The working people of the Kulunda Regional Center could not watch indifferently the antisocial doings of the Baptists. The community of the region assembled in the House of Culture. Four hundred people attended. They summoned Subbotin, the preacher. He approached the rostrum firmly and self-assuredly, pretending calmness. In short, by his behavior, he wanted to show the people that he was ready to accept all trials and tribulations for his faith. Obviously, for this reason, when giving his explanations, he applied many dishonest measures: he pretended not to understand, he lied, avoided direct answers and dodged.

"Why did you not register your sect?" he was asked.

"They don't register," said Subbotin hypocritically. "Our representative went there . . . we wrote to Moscow . . ."

When he was told that that "representative" did not turn anywhere, Subbotin, puzzled, made a helpless gesture:

"I did not know it."

It was obvious to everybody that the pastor was cunning and inconsistent. It was disclosed at the meeting that the sectarians did not respect State order or the rules of socialist community life.

Judge for yourselves. It suffices Subbotin to come home and make a dissatisfied face, to make his wife fall to the ground like a mown sheaf. In what way has he achieved this? In a simple way—by tyranny. He beats up his children and makes his wife kneel down for punishment.

"Do you know that, under our laws, tortures and tyranny are severely punished?" he was asked at the meeting.

"Well, I neither torture nor tyrannize them," the pastor explained. "Simply, for their own good, for educational purposes, I take the switch from time to time. It is allowed and necessary to use a switch. . . ."

Obviously [he had] a cross on his chest and switches in his hand. Therefore, the framed signs in Subbotin's home: "God is love" and "Take your burdens to the Lord," look ridiculous and hypocritical. By the way, Subbotin's son reproduced these signs with his camera. Then these numerous sayings, which the pastor himself rudely violated, were distributed in the city of Frunze among the members of the same community, as well as in other cities.

For Subbotin, the meeting turned out to be a bitter pill. It was necessary to reply to the questions impressively and convincingly, without injury to his pastoral dignity. What, for example, could he say concerning secret meetings at three or four o'clock in the morning?

"We do not assemble at 4 a.m.," was all that the pastor was able to say. It came out that they had their meetings at 2 a.m. But is there a big difference?

The community of the Kulunda Regional Center decided: to ask the Prosecutor to initiate a criminal case against the most active members of the Baptist community.

* * *

There appeared before the Court as defendants: Feokrit Ivanovich Subbotin, Liubov Michailovna Khmara and the brothers Nikolai Kuzmich Khmara and Vasilii Kuzmich Khmara. The trial lasted four days. For four days the collective of the judges of the Altai Country Court painstakingly investigated the case of the Kulunda sect.

The defendants pleaded not guilty, having declared that they did not commit any crime, then refused to testify on the essence of the charges.

They carefully withheld from the Court the contents of their sermons at the meetings. However, the testimony of witnesses and the evidence gathered during the investigation proved that, by dragging minors into their group, they brought them up in a separation of the communal life, called upon the believers to refuse to fulfill their public obligations, incited the believers to disobey the *druzhinniki*, to refuse to join labor unions and, in general, to abstain from any public activity. The prayers were conducted illegally, at nighttime, in unsanitary conditions and with the participation of minors. The chief sanitary physician of the Kulunda Region came to the conclusion that the premises in which the prayers were conducted were not fit for meetings (there was not the required volume of air, the ventilation was not available, etc.).

Prolonged prayers in such rooms adversely affected healthy people, especially children.

The trial also brought to light the prehistory of the creation of this community. At Kulunda there existed for a long time an unregistered community of believing Evangelical Christian Baptists. This community preached the Bible and performed religious practices in accordance with the statutes of the All-Union Council of the Evangelical Christian Baptists (V.S.E.K.H.B.). From 1961 on, all kinds of appeals, communiqués and other texts criticizing V.S.E.K.H.B. started to appear among believing Baptists. Since that time, the activities of a portion of the community have been of a reactionary character.

In November 1962 the Chairman of the Settlement Council of Kulunda tried either to register the Community or to terminate its activities.

The old people complied, but the younger members of the community, with Subbotin at their head, separated. They started illegal meetings at nighttime. This group of the believers refused to recognize the official status of the V.S.E.K.H.B. and got out from under the control of the Laws concerning religious cults, which are in force in the U.S.S.R.

Subbotin organized an illegal school for the training of young Baptists. After the schooling, examinations were held on the basis of questionnaires which included such questions as: "On what day did God create man?" Yet the question: on what day was it that the activities of the Community became harmful to our State, to our society, to the people, including the believers themselves, did not interest Subbotin at all.

The tribunal in charge of criminal matters, of the Altai Country Court, sentenced the organizer of the Kulunda group of the reactionarily disposed Baptists, Subbotin, to five years in prison, the brothers, N. Khmara and V. Khmara, to three years in prison, and in consideration of the circumstances mitigating the responsibility, imposed a conditional sentence on Mrs. L. Khmara.

Simultaneously, the Country Court passed down a decision under Civil Law by which it submitted to the Kulunda Regional Executive Committee of the Soviet workers the question of a possible transfer of the upbringing of minor children of those sentenced to youth institutions. They should grow to become builders of Communism and not moral freaks.

The Supreme Court of the Russian S.F.S.R. upheld the sentence.

V. Tonkikh

Source: *Sovetskaia Justitsia* (Soviet Justice), No. 10, May 1964, pp. 12 ff.

26

Crimes Against Persons and Citizens' Rights Committed by Religious Groups

Commentary on the Criminal Code of the Russian S.F.S.R.

Encroachments on the rights and interests of Soviet citizens, no matter under what pretext or in what form they are executed, present a considerable social danger and are recognized in Criminal Law as crimes. Even cases of encroachment on persons and rights of citizens committed in the form of the propagation of religious beliefs and performance of religious rites are not excluded from this rule.

Section 227, Criminal Code, of the Russian S.F.S.R. (Socialist Federative Soviet Republic), establishes responsibility for organizing or leading a group, the activities of which, undertaken under the pretext of the propagation of religious beliefs and the performance of religious rites, are connected with inflicting harm to the health of citizens, with the encroachment on the person or any rights of citizens or with inciting citizens to abstain from participation in community activities or from the performance of citizen's duties, as well as with the engagement of minors in the activities of such group.

The crime referred to in Section 227, Criminal Code, of the Russian S.F.S.R., inflicts harm to many social relations; *the performance of fanatical rites hurts the believers physically and morally and is essentially harmful to the health of the citizens. The inducement of believers to abstain from community activities infringes on the political right of citizens and on the orderly fulfillment of citizens' duties.* Finally, the *social danger of the activities of this type of religious groups is expressed in the fact that it is often connected with the engagement of minors in their activities, and that these groups constitute a shelter for adventurers and parasites who live at the expense of the believers.*

The objective aspect of the offense provided in Paragraph 1, Section 227, may be expressed either in the fact of organization of such group, or in the leadership of such group.

A group (in the meaning of Section 227, Criminal Code) is a religious organization (including a religious sect) the activities of which, conducted under the pretext of the propagation of religious teachings or the performance of religious practices, is connected with the encroachment on the person and rights of citizens. In this respect, it is of no importance as to whether such a religious association under whose name such group exists (Evangelic Christian Baptist; Seventh Day Adventists) may be registered or whether its activities are directly forbidden by Law (Witnesses of Jehovah, *Piatidesiatniki, Khlists, Innokentievtsi* and others).

The *majority of the believers appear to be cheated, to be victims of criminal activities of sectarian preachers.* Therefore, one should not assume that the rank-and-file participants of religious congregations (groups) are united for the purpose of committing crimes. Even more so, these groups should not be regarded as criminal associations (criminal sects) for this reason only, that in their midst, criminals are busy, encroaching on the persons and rights of the believers. In consideration of the above, *only organizers (leaders) and active participants* in such religious groups—

persons truly guilty of crime, and not rank-and-file believers, *can be made criminally responsible* for the commitment of the deeds listed in Section 227.

Organizing of a group—is the creation of any religious association with the purpose, under the pretext of religious activities, *to execute acts which inflict harm on the health of citizens* or is connected with other encroachments on the person or rights of citizens. *The organizer of a group—is a person who* formed a religious association (*appointed preachers, recruited believers to the sect, provided the group with literature, prepared plans for its activities, etc.*). *It is not at all required that the organizer participates* in the subsequent activities of the group which he had formed. For example, there are known wandering preachers who spread some religious teachings in various parts of the country.

Some sectarian "authorities" are only engaged in organizational activities concerning the formation of illegal groups in various places, and then execute a general leadership from one religious center.

Thus, in 1961, one of the leaders of the sect of the Piatidesiatniki, *Prokhorov, was made to stand trial, because, for many years, he was systematically active organizing sectarian groups. He formed several congregations. He placed specially selected preachers at the head of each of these congregations.*

During the prayer meetings of the sectarians, the leaders of the above-mentioned congregations, Korytko, Khomiakov *and others, referred to evangelical commandments and called upon the believers not to be carried away by* "worldly matters," not to take part in social life, not to attend theaters or movies, not to read Soviet literature. As a result of all this, Citizen N., born in 1944, was driven to fanaticism and stopped attending school. Two girls left the *Komsomol* and ceased to attend cultural and educational programs.

Prokhorov was sentenced, under Paragraph 1, Section 227, Criminal Code of the Russian S.F.S.R., to five years' deprivation of freedom.

Leadership of a group is determined by such acts of persons heading a given group as carrying out of illegal assemblies at which the sectarians are told about the necessity of refusal to participate in social activities or to fulfill citizen's duties; *preparation and carrying out of wild fanatical rites of the sect (baptism with "the Holy Spirit" or by "Holy Water," etc.); recruiting of new members of the sect, including minors, etc.*

It should be stressed that the leaders of the group (sect) may engage in the above-mentioned criminal activities not only during the (prayer) meetings but also by *individually influencing the believers.*

It has no bearing on the composition of the crime, in what way the leader of the group makes the believers fulfill their religious commandments and participate in the activities of the group (threatening, scaring or cheating).

The activities of the leader of the sectarian group of the so-called group of "Christians of Evangelical Faith," Korytko, can serve as an example of the leadership of one of these groups.

In order to excite religious fanaticism among the believers, *Korytko organized systematically, four times a week, illegal meetings of the sectarians, which* had a rather gloomy character and *were accompanied by shouts and visual and hearing hallucinations.* During the mass hysteria, the believers made incoherent sounds, trembled, cried and asked the "Holy Spirit" to fulfill their wishes. Some believers even lost consciousness.

Korytko was sentenced under Paragraph 1, Section 227, Criminal Code, R.S.F.S.R., to deprivation of freedom.

Subject to criminal responsibility under Paragraph 1, Section 227, Criminal Code, are the leaders and organizers of any such group, the activities of which, carried out under the pretext of religious rites and teachings, are connected with the particular [criminal] effects stated by law.

1. Causing harm to the health of citizens is characteristic of the activities of several fanatical sects *(Piatidesiatniki, Khlysts, Innokentievtsi, Skoptsi, etc.). The harm to the health of the believers can be inflicted, on the one hand, in the process of the praying itself (zealotry), by long-lasting fasts,* or refusal to accept medical assistance, and on the other hand, as a result of *sacrifices which they regard as a payment for the "absolution of sins."* In the first case, the believers, being under the impact of abnormal surroundings, bring themselves to a harmful health condition. In this situation, *the role of the sectarian preachers is* limited to a psychological influence on the believers and to *carrying the process of praying to a heated state.*

In consideration of the above, the activity of the leaders of religious groups (fanatical sects) is qualified not as offenses against the person but, rather, as those provided by Paragraph 1, Section 227, Criminal Code, R.S.F.S.R.

By analogy, the question of the responsibility of the organizers and leaders of sects should be decided, in case their sect numbers inflict harm upon their own health as a result of fasting and refusal to accept medical assistance.

In the Court practice, there are frequent cases where a decision has to be made as to the qualification of the acts of sectarians, who, carrying out the orders of their leaders, refuse to take their sick relatives to a hospital and do not call the physician but hope for the "power of God." In our opinion, such acts should be qualified as active participation in the activities of a fanatical group (Paragraph 2, Section 227, Criminal Code, and corresponding sections of the chapter dealing with offenses against the person), depending upon the circumstances of the deed, such as intentional killing, or unintentional, one resulting from omission.

If the sect leaders, in the process of performing religious rites, intentionally inflict bodily harm on the believer (for example, castration of the believers in the sect of *Skoptsi*), or to cause his death (the rite of burying alive in the sect of the *Innokentievtsitatunisti*) they are subject to criminal responsibility for a compounds offense under Paragraph 1, Section 227, Criminal Code, R.S.F.S.R., and a corresponding section of the chapter dealing with offenses against the person (intentional serious bodily injury, intentional killing).

The attempt to characterize such fanatical rite of some sects as the act of sacrifice brings about several legal questions.

The panel of judges for criminal cases, of the Supreme Court of the R.S.F.S.R., in its decision of June 1, 1961, in the case against Fedotov, Afonin, Kalinina and others, pointed out that the act of the leaders and preachers of a religious sect, who incited people they had recruited to their sect to commit suicide, should be considered under Section 107 (causing other people's suicide) and Section 227, Criminal Code, R.S.F.S.R. (see "Bulletin of the Supreme Court R.S.F.S.R.," 1961, No. 4, pp. 8-9).

The above-mentioned persons, being leaders and preachers of an illegal sect of the *Piatidesiatniki*, systematically conducted meetings and prayers with the sectarians, which were accompanied by fanatical rites that drove people to a frenzy.

Afonin and Kalinina, in their preachings and in their talk with the believer, Mrs. K., propagated the idea that, "for the sake of eternal life and our Lord," one should accept any sacrifice. As a result, Mrs. K. attempted to throw her minor daughter in front of an automobile. Driven to a state of depression, she ended her life by suicide, having thrown herself before a moving train. In the same way, the believer, Mrs. N., was moved to commit suicide.

If the leaders of a sect, under the pretext of religious activities, instigate believers to kill their relatives, their deeds should be qualified as compound offenses—as instigation to killing and leadership of a fanatical sect.

The leader of the same sectarian group, Fedotov, along with driving some of the believers to suicide, required the rank-and-file sectarians, for the sake of the absolution of "heavy sins," to sacrifice their children. Thus, on July 21, 1960, he summoned Citizen K., charged her with the revealing of the secrets of the sect, and ordered her to kill her daughter. Only due to the fact that Mrs. K. told other believers about it, the monstrous crime was prevented.

By the decision of the Moscow District Court of April 26, 1961, Afonin and Kalinina were sentenced under Section 107 and Section 227, Criminal Code, R.S.F.S.R., and the sect leader, Fedotov, also under Section 17, and under Section 136a, Criminal Code, R.S.F.S.R., of 1926, to various terms in prison.

2. Other encroachments on the person or rights of citizens may consist of locking up the believers in isolated apartments, depriving them of liberty; encouraging them to sexual lewdness (the sect of *Khlysts*); *prohibiting marriage with nonbelievers,* the use of Soviet money, acceptance of support and retirement pensions, attending movies and theaters, reading newspapers, having children educated in schools, etc.

3. The instigation of the citizens to refuse to participate in social activities or to fulfill citizens' duties, as one of the characteristics of the criminal activity of the organizers and leaders of religious sects, may consist of various acts: the prohibiting of the believers to take part in social life (attend meetings and assemblies, participate in festive demonstrations); *instigating the believers to refuse to join*

Labor Unions and other public organizations or forcing them to leave them: prohibiting the believers from participating in the elections to the Soviets of workers' deputies and to other representative bodies; encouraging the believers not to work at the enterprises and *kolkhozi* [collective farms], not to pay taxes, etc.

4. The drawing of minors into the group may be carried out both by the leaders and by other members of the sect.

The drawing of minors into the group by organizers and leaders of those groups is considered under Paragraph 1, Section 227, Criminal Code, R.S.F.S.R., and by other active members—according to Paragraph 2 of the same section. This is so, because Paragraph 1, Section 227, provides for criminal responsibility not for the drawing of minors into the group, as an independent offense, but, rather, for organizing and leading a group, the activity of which is connected with the above-mentioned acts. The ways of drawing minors into a group may be different (convincing, fraud, threat, beating, etc.). It has no bearing on the characteristic of the crime, whether or not the minors were relatives of the perpetrator.

The *drawing into a group requires, first of all, making the minors participate in its activities (presence at illegal meetings, participation in prayers and executing religious rites, etc.).* A religious education of a minor at home, as far as it is not connected with the drawing of the minor into the group, does not constitute the above offense.

It is not required for an offense as provided in Section 227, Criminal Code, R.S.F.S.R., to be considered as accomplished, that, as the result of the activities of the organizer or leader of the group, the effects indicated in the law, be present. The fact that such a group has been formed suffices.

Paragraph 2, Section 227, Criminal Code, R.S.F.S.R., provides for criminal responsibility for active participation in the activities of the group, including systematic propaganda aimed at the committing by the group members of acts directed against the person or the rights of citizens.

The active participation in the activities of a group may be expressed by the drawing into it of new members, including minors, by the fulfillment of the particular orders of the leaders (execution of the rite of "baptism by water," supplying of religious literature, claiming to be a "prophet," etc.), *by providing room for illegal meetings, by collecting financial means among the believers, etc.*

A systematic propaganda, aiming at the commitment of deeds listed in Paragraph 1, Section 227, Criminal Code, R.S.F.S.R., consists of more than one case of dissemination of all kind of religious ideas which could inspire the believers to refuse to participate in social activities and to fulfill their citizen's duties, as well as to commit acts which cause harm to the health of people. It has no bearing on the presence of essential characteristics of the crime, or in what form (orally or in writing) this propaganda is executed.

The crime is considered as accomplished the moment when the above-mentioned acts are executed, regardless of how the citizens reacted to them. If harmful effects resulted from such propaganda, they should be considered as aggravating circumstances and should constitute reasons for the application to the guilty person of more severe punishment.

It should be pointed out that the criminal responsibility extends not only to active participants in illegal sects whose activities are generally forbidden by law but also to those religious groups (sects) which, not being forbidden, however, use their existence for the commission of acts which are harmful to the health of the citizens, for instigating the believers to refuse to participate in social activities or to fulfill their citizen's duties, or for other encroachments on the rights and interests of the citizens.

The subjective aspect of the offense in question is expressed in intentional guilt. The organizer and the leader of a group, as well as its active participants, recognize the social danger of their acts, especially, that they are connected with inciting the citizens to refuse to participate in social activities and to fulfill their citizen's duties, or with the drawing of minors into their group; that they foresee the dangerous effects of their deeds and intend for them to come about.

As far as such effects as inflicting harm on the health of the citizens, guilt may appear both in the form of intent and of negligence. If the perpetrator indirectly causes grave harm to the health of the injured or causes his death, his deed should be qualified as a compound offense under Section 227, Criminal Code, R.S.F.S.R., and corresponding provisions of the chapter dealing with offenses against the person.

Religious fanaticism, advantages or other base reasons

can constitute motives for the commission of the given crime.

The note to Section 227, Criminal Code, R.S.F.S.R., explains that if the acts of the persons mentioned in Part Two of this section, or the persons who committed them, do not present a major social danger, social educational measures can be applied. The question as to whether the given act and the person who committed it constitute a serious social danger should be resolved in every separate case in consideration of all circumstances accompanying the commission of the deed.

Being relieved from criminal responsibility and penalty, as mentioned above, does not constitute a complete absence of responsibility of persons who committed a socially dangerous act. In such cases a substitution of criminal responsibility by social educational measures takes place. The provisions of Law, included in the note to Section 227, Criminal Code, R.S.F.S.R., give the opportunity on a broad basis to engage the society in the struggle against the antisocial activities of the religious sects, to prevent the commission of crimes and to conduct an extensive educational work directed toward the removal of religious prejudices from the consiousness of people.

M. Mikhailov
Iu. Milko

Source: *Komsomolskaia Pravda*, May 22, 1964, p. 4

27

Black and Red

(Reason against religion)

Outside the windows, electric wires sang a fearful song. A storm was gathering. Early darkness came heavily upon the earth. . . .

Sadness came over my mind. But, mind you, it was not so much because of the weather, but rather due to the tragic human story which they told me a while ago.

On the couch, in front of me, a little boy sat and enthusiastically turned the pages of a book with his ink-stained fingers. Nothing on his face reflected the recent tragedy. There was just a hint of sadness. . . .

I could hardly believe that *this fifth grader, Kolia Sviridov, was the same boy whom the charlatans with crosses on their chests had declared to be a "saint"* and "successor of the Emperor."

Kolia had no childhood and did not know his parents, although they lived nearby. *He was a "God's child"* and a God's child must not have parents on earth. *In his early years, Kolia was taken away from his mother and given for upbringing to "sisters"—nuns.* Such was God's will. . . .

At six o'clock every morning, the one-eyed grandmother, Agrafena, would wake up the boy—and make him pray. Her fingers were bony and hard like the fire tongs which she used to put charcoal into the samovar. . . .

Grandmother Agrafena was regarded as the senior among the "sisters." *She was the first one to go down on her knees in front of the private iconostasis and, more ardently than all the others, she would make the bows all the way to the floor. She loved God more than the others.* Maybe God loved her, too, and Kolia was wondering: how is it possible to love such a wicked old woman?

In summer they sometimes allowed the boy to go outside on the street—early in the morning or late at night so that nobody could "cast a spell" on the "holy" child. The cold dew of the grass made his bare feet cold (monks do not wear shoes).

There was fog rolling in the thicket on the river bank—soft, warm and humid, like hot milk that you could spoon out and drink. The boy wanted to stay awhile on the street, but the merciless Agrafena took him by his shoulder with her hard hands and led him back into the mud hut. Such was God's will. . . .

In the cell of the child, in the corner behind the big clay oven, there hung old valuable icons of the Holy Mother and other saints. The paint on the icons was cracked from age and had become dark; Kolia had the impression that the eyes of the Mother of God were walleyed. For some reason they reminded him of Agrafena.

The old people demanded that the boy should love God; but Kolia did not love God and was scared of Him.

The boy walked with his head down, stooped, feeling the heavy burden of constant fear upon him. Kolia would want to be a normal boy, to run around, to play and laugh. But he was supposed to remain the "holy successor to the Emperor." Such was God's will. . . .

God proved to be cruel and demanding. He took away the son from Petr and Praskoviia Sviridov. Also for the sake of Jesus Christ, Evodikiia Svididova, a distant relative of Kolia's father, entered the *underground monastery* under the leadership of Grandmother Agrafena.

God had made dozens of people who had built their mud houses on the banks of the Temirtau reservoir to separate themselves with walls of icons from the outer world. A few kilometers away from these mud houses, nightly fires were burning in the first furnaces of the Kazakhstanskaia *Magnitka* plant, but here, *crowded in tight groups, people were praying by the flickering light of small candles.* God forbade work, threatening to render the "culprits" into the hands of the Satan. God would not permit children to attend the school of the "Antichrist," because they did not teach there "the laws of God."

It was God that forbade Petr Sviridov and his brother, Valentin, at an hour of national emergency, to take up arms in the defense of the country against the enemies.

But, by the way, all this pleased not only God alone. . . .

The believers were told to abandon worldly life, to refuse to recognize the Soviet Government and its laws but, rather, patiently to wait for the return of Emperor Nicholas II or his successor. *"God wanted"* them to remain *"truly orthodox Christians,"* devoted with their bodies and souls to Him alone and to His *"chosen"* one—*the Emperor of Russia.*

Acting as "God's mouthpiece," the preachers announced Kolia, the newly born son of Petr and Praskoviia, to be the "successor to the Emperor," and locked him in the underground monastery.

The news of the appearance of the "holy child" at Temirtau spread to sectarian centers in other cities. Believers from Karaganda moved here. *The illegal monastery filled with new monks. Leaving her family, one Ekaterinu Lernikova came to Temirtau and took her vows as a nun.*

In the tiny settlement near Temirtau, they tried to use the boy for the purposes of arousing religious fanaticism.

The Cheka [political police] members found Kolia. In a black robe of a monk, the seven-year-old boy sat in his corner behind the oven, pale and tiny like a potato plant grown in a cellar. An old lamp was hanging above his head. In this underground monastery, the agents of State Security found, in a secret hiding place, about two thousand old Tsarist rubles. The "sisters in Christ" had preserved them for over forty years. . . .

In August 1960, a Comrade's Court convened in the Cultural Center of the workers of metallurgy. *The Court decided to deport six most active sectarian parasites to distant regions of the Soviet Union* for their refusal to engage in a socially useful work. Truly, they deserved to be judged with all the severity of our Law. But people who believe in the future and whom the truth of life makes strong are usually human.

The People's Court approved the decision of the Comrade's Court concerning the deportation of the leaders of the sect and *deprived Petr and Praskoviia Sviridov of the paternal rights.* The people did not take away the child from the parents—because they had abandoned the child long ago; people took it from the demanding and cruel "God" who stole from the little boy more than one-half of his childhood.

It is easy to put Kolia into a children's home, in a boarding school or even in a sanatorium. He can get his shoes, clothing, food and a desk in the classroom. *But children are happy only when they feel the warmth of paternal care, when they can call somebody—even not aloud—their father and mother.*

An official pursuit of duty brought together Kolia and Captain Khutornoi. It was he, Roman Iakovlevich Khutornoi, who visited the settlement near Temirtau, met relatives and friends of the sectarians until he found Kolia in the underground monastery.

A few days before the Court session, Captain Khutornoi came to visit the youth.

"He is playing and running around somewhere," the stern Grandmother Agrafena said while *she continued to cross herself.*

Roman Iakovlevich entered the foreroom, looked

around with an experienced eye and soon brought the boy out of the cellar.

"What are you doing here?"

"I am Kolia, the Holy Monk ..." The boy started to answer the way he was trained.

"Don't bother," Khutornoi stopped him. "I know everything. I know that you are the successor to the Emperor and I am the Antichrist. . . . What do you think, do I really look like the Antichrist. . . ?" The Captain smiled and put his hand on Kolia's shoulder.

Kolia completely forgot the grandmother's advice that, at the sight of the Antichrist, one should make the sign of a cross and that, in general one should not get close and let him touch you. With a mixture of fear and curiosity, he watched the man who knew in advance what he was about to say.

"If you want, I'll drive you in an automobile," Roman Iakovlevich suggested.

The boy quickly approached the car and sat next to the driver. . . .

All evening, Kolia had to kneel and pray for forgiveness of his "sin" against God. At night, he was dreaming of the shiny *Pobeda* [make of the car]. Through the windshield the happy eyes of the new acquaintance were looking at him.

It was probably at that time that the friendship between the two was born, a friendship chary of cordiality, shy and touchy. Or, perhaps, it happened later, when the boy became an inmate of the children's home.

Kolia slowly adjusted to the children's collective. He avoided bright boys and looked down upon the girls. The sectarians had firmly put into his mind the idea that "a woman is not worthy of any attention of the Holy Monk."

In his free time, Kolia hid in a corner, read or secretly prayed to God. He read well and learned to write quickly. At the request of Captain Khutornoi, he was transferred to the second grade.

Having himself been in the past an inmate of a children's home, and having a hard life behind him, Roman Iakovlevich visited the children's home nearly every day. Naturally, giving his free time to a "strange" boy, teaching him to play and to laugh, all this was not a part of the official duties of the Captain of State Security, Khutornoi.

But, apparently, it is not so easy to always see where the official duty ends and humanity begins. . . .

In the fall, *Kolia fell sick. The physicians found myocarditis*—an inflammation of the myocardium. The boy was hospitalized. The young lady doctor, Andreeva, had some twenty patients. Now there was one more, a special one. He was the "quietest." *He never complained, never played or laughed.* He accepted the kindness of the grownups with hesitation and suspicion.

Kolia "opened his mind" only to Captain Khutornoi and to the senior nurse of the hospital, Valentina Fedorovna Karnaukhova. He boasted before other boys with "his Captain." And the nurse—she apparently became more than just a nurse to him, but a mother, too.

The boy had many adult friends. Several times he was visited by the Secretary of the Oktiabrskii Regional Committee of *Komsomol*, Georgii Shestakov. Strange children came to see him, girls would bring him sweets. "Strange" teachers would come to teach him right there in his hospital room. . . .

Kolia spent his winter vacation with Roman Iakovlevich Khutornoi's family. For the second semester he transferred to a boarding school. . . .

This winter I visited again the boarding school in which Kolia attends the fifth grade. I talked to the school director, N. A. Chepurina, and to Kolia's first teacher, a young pedagogue, S. A. Bocharoba. She now teaches the fifth grade and I asked her to take me to the classes.

There were many pupils eager to tell about the religion of the ancient Greeks. The teacher called Kolia.

"The ancient Greeks invented gods because they could not explain the phenomena of the nature. . . ."

Kolia talked about Zeus the Thunderer, about Prometheus who stole fire from the gods and gave it to people. I listened to him and thought of other things. How much work and effort, how much kindness and humaneness was needed on the part of the teachers to warm up the frozen heart of the boy, to give him back his childhood and to inflame his soul with the beautiful sparks of Prometheus' fire. . . .

The teachers told me about Kolia's first meeting with his mother. Praskoviia Alekseevna came to the school with Aunt Niura, her relative on her husband's side.

The boy talked to the aunt, paying no attention to the strange woman.

"Kolia, don't you know me?" his mother decided to ask.

"Who is this, Aunt Niura?"

Praskoviia Alekseevna's face twisted and trembled. She blinked her eyes again and again. *Heavy tears rolled down her face* and fell on the nun's black robe. Perhaps these tears of the mother who lost her son washed away from her eyes the unseen curtain and she could see her son again —alive, worldly, real. She saw the world, the earth, the people who, not for Christ's sake but for life's sake, have been taking care of this "strange," but dear to them, boy.

Temirtau
A. Bogachuk,
Our correspondent

Source: *Sovetskaia Latviia*, June 18, 1964

28

Wild Fanatics

From the Courtroom:

Recently, the assizes of the People's Court of the Balvskii Region tried the criminal case against the organizers and active participants of a group of the sect of the Piatidesiat-niki, *I. Koltsov, Mrs. E. Koltsov and P. Liepinsh.* The activity of this sect has brought harm to the health of the people. Also, the sectarians instigated people to refuse to fulfill their citizen's duties.

The testimony of the defendants and witnesses uncovered to those present in the courtroom the loathsome and fanatical character of the rites performed by the sect of the *Pentecostals.*

How were the prayers conducted in this sect?

The defendant, P. Liepinsh, testified:

"We gathered together, got down on all fours and started barking like dogs. This is how we turned to God. It was like in a madhouse."

Liepinsh's story was supplemented by the witnesses Pommers, Ositis, Didin and others, who testified that, during the prayers, people looked insane, leaped like rabbits, howled and made senseless sounds. *Incidentally, one of the meetings took place in Koltsov's pigsty.*

Equally hysterical shouts accompanied the "baptisms" which were arranged by the leader of the sect, Koltsov. *Half-undressed men and women would immerse in the water in the pit which is usually used by the local kolkhoz as a silage for the cattle.*

These wild orgies could not remain without an ill effect upon the health of the people. One of the first victims of these inhuman rites of the *Pentecostals* was Elena Koltsova, a sister of the sect's leader. For several years she suffered from tuberculosis. The woman was many times instructed to enter the tuberculosis dispensary, and several times physicians came to her home to give her medical help.

But Koltsov convinced his sister that, if she joined the sect and performed all the rites, she would be delivered from her illness. The sick woman believed him, joined the sect and started avoiding the physicians. The sectarians subjected Miss E. Koltsov to the "baptism" in cold water and made her regularly perform the fanatical rites. This eventually ruined her health and soon she died.

The fanatical performance of the rites nearly deprived of life another member of the sect, Petr Liepinsh. He was saved by his brother Ianis who, against the will of the sectarian, took him to the hospital. Immediate surgery saved Petr's life.

The leader of the sect categorically forbade the "brothers in Christ" to attend meetings or movies, to listen to radio, to read newspapers, books and magazines. All this was pronounced as a great sin. On various pretenses, they told the believers to avoid service in the Soviet Army.

The fanatics would not stop at any means to drag people into their sect. Threats and direct force were applied. *When the sect leader, I. Koltsov, saw that he was not able to lure Ianis Liepinsh into the sect he announced that "the Holy Spirit" ordered the obstinate one to be killed or burned to death. Ianis, persecuted by the* Piatidesiatniki, *was forced*

*not to stay at home at night and to hide in his neighbors'
homes.*

In our country, the fight against the grave survival in
people's minds—religion, is conducted by way of patient
enlightenment concerning the inconsistencies of the religious creeds, and by propagation of the scientific and
technological achievements. However, we are not permitted
to hurt the religious feelings of the believers, in this
connection. On the other hand, the laws which protect the
rights of the Soviet people do not allow the infringement
upon the person of a citizen and upon his health. The
sectarians ignored these laws.

It was only the interference of the administrative organs
that put an end to the criminal activity of the sect of the
Piatidesiatniki in the town of Rugai. The leader of the sect,
I. Koltsov, was sentenced to five years in prison. Also,
according to their merits, other sect leaders were sentenced. But can we end the story here?

This whole story makes us think of many things. Did not
the sect act illegally and criminally for too long a period of
time? Where had the militant atheists been? Apparently
they did not pay the necessary attention to the educational
atheistic propaganda at Rugai. It was not without reason
that the Community Prosecutors, comrades who participated in the trial, Trepsha and Stradynia, stressed this
matter.

The Court trial against the leaders of the sect of the
Piatidesiatniki should serve as a significant lesson to
the Party, *Komsomol* and other social organizations of the
Balvskii Region. They should undertake every measure in
order to better the atheistic propaganda work among the
population and persistently educate people in the material-
istic philosophy of life.

S. Zhilinskii,
Prosecutor of the Balvskii Region

1965

Source: *Selskaia Zhizn* (Village Life), February 13, 1965, p. 4

29

Those Who Spread Darkness

The belief of a superstitious man in mysteries and ghosts does not make sense. It prevents him from being an active builder of a new society and looking at the world with bright eyes. You can read about it in many letters to the editors. Here are some of them.

"Sidor Pliukhin, from the village of Chumakovo near Novosibirsk, reads his Bible from the early morning," I. Fedotov writes, "and then he hurries to earn money as a carpenter in the nearby village. He knocks with the butt of his axe at the rotten parts of a house and tells the owner:

"Well, the poor house asks to be repaired. . . ."

"People are shocked by the amount of money he charges, but Pliukhin is all smiles when he replies:

"The price is simply divine."

"Resourceful Akulina, his wife, also knows now to catch her prey. As soon as she sees a girl overcome by sadness, she displays cards in front of her and starts her mysterious talk. "Well, your sweetheart loves you no more. But do not worry, I am going to help you." Then she goes into whisper: "I know a good medicine, just come to me with a gift."

"Hope rises in the girl's heart, she hurries to see the sorceress. Akulina obviously fools around: she either scares the gullible girl or consoles her. . . . And, if her attempt to gain profit fails, she gets in a rage:

"'I am going to frame you, you will howl in front of me.'"

The fanaticism of the bigot coincides with dirty tricks. As reader A. Barshchevakii writes to the editor: "There lives in the village of Kurmysh near Kazan a Tatiana Sharonova-Kuvaeva. Long ago she traded her conscience for greediness, abandoned honest work and profits from human plight.

" 'One mass for the dead is not enough,' she blasphemes. 'The soul of the dead will lament.'

"Trusting people order *panakhida* services from her again and again. And she, *having grabbed a bag of crosses and icons* [*holy pictures*] *goes out to the villages to trade them.*"

Some spreaders of obscurity propagate the rubbish about the "holy water," the charcoal and other superstitions not in good faith, others because of their stupidity.

"The following happened in the village of Starino near Cherepovets," A. Fomichev reports. "There is one well—the water went bad."

" 'Did you pour the holy water into it?' Matrena, an old woman, asked the village dwellers.

" 'Yes, we did, yesterday.'

" 'Did you remove the smell?'

" 'No, we didn't.'

"Matrena poured the 'holy water' again and again. After three days, the well was cleaned and the water became clear, pleasing to the taste.

" 'Well, the "holy water" helped,' Matrena insists."

A dying woman was brought from her house to the hospital. The surgeon performed the operation, saved the patient's life. The superstitious woman now insists that, apparently, God Himself let her live for the sake of her children. This fact is reported with dismay by Ludmila Shchitova of the village of Krasnii kardon in the province of Tselinograd.

The priests and all kind of other charlatans infest the minds of the gullible people the way a burdock infests the field.

Mrs. K. Glazkova, a teacher from the village of N. Ilderiakovo near Kazan, A. Bilina from the village of Srub near Nezhin and many other readers report that superstition firmly persists only in those places where it is regarded as something entirely harmless.

N. Akulinichev writes that, in the village of Narishkino, Tulskaia Province, even the local church choir member, Evgenia Kosova reproaches the atheists. "Formerly, it was gay and interesting in our club; I myself used to sing in the club's choir. Now the club is often locked, there is hardly any activity carried on there." Well, so now she sings in the church.

So far, superstitions of all colors and shades are still

alive. Therefore, we have no right to forget or weaken the propaganda of scientific atheism. It is not fitting that the atheists keep "quieter than water and lower than grass."

V. Parfenov

Source: *Selskaia Zhizn* (Village Life), May 13, 1965, p. 4

30

Reason Against Dope

Considering the letters to the editor:

"My father was a believing man. And the more he believed in God, the more sins he had," writes Grigorii Dmitrievich Koniakhin, a resident of the village of Frukto-voc, Bakhchisarai Region in the Crimea Oblast (Province). In his letter, Grigorii Dmitrievich tells the story of his life, a life hard and bitter, memories of longlasting and tiresome disputes and searching for the real truth: in what surrounds us or in religion, in the teaching of the Bible or the Gospel. . . . The enlightenment finally came, but not soon and not easily at all. After the teachers in his school had planted in his mind a spark of doubt in religion and inspired him with the love of his country, the years of the Fatherland War made the volunteer soldier Koniakhin ask himself again and again: "If God is so merciful, why does He allow millions of people to perish from the hands of the Fascists?"

Grigorii Dimitrievich concluded his letter-revelation with these notable lines:

"It is painful to realize that there are still people among us who believe in the biblical fairy tales! I am now broadening my general education, though it is sometimes difficult to catch up on what was neglected during the years of youth."

Incidentally, the letter from the village of Fruktovoc is

not at all an exception in the voluminous mail coming to our editor. It has become a habit with our Soviet people that, whether they gain victory or suffer failure, they wish to present it to the people for their judgment, to hear their good advice or just criticism.

"I have found that any religion is an opiate for people," P. Zilitinkevich, a former priest of the Crimean *sovkhoz, Vinogradni*, writes. "Naturally, it was not all of a sudden that I decided to disfrock and admit my guilt in cheating the believers. But, finally, I did this, too, and I think that I did the right thing."

And here is another letter which calls for consideration. The author of the letter is N. Sokolov, Chairman of the *kolkhoz, Rossiia*, Tutaievskii Region in the Province of Iaroslavl. He asks the editors and the readers for their advice concerning what he should do. And the story told by the *kolkhoz* Chairman is quite interesting. *There is a church in their village. There is the family of the priest with two children in school. So, one day these children came to school with crosses around their necks.* The community was indignant. They tried to convince the parents—without success. Then *they forbade the priest's children to attend school.* The parents filed a complaint. The Chairman of the Regional Department of Education gave an explanation: the Law on general education may not be violated, the children should attend school.

Well, the story that happened was not a pleasant one. But, after all, who is responsible for it? Surely, the Chairman of the Regional Department is right. Nobody has the right to violate the Law on the general compulsory education. Regardless of the parents, the children are, first of all, our Soviet children. These children are to live in our society; together with all others and arm in arm with them, they will build and form this society. What is important is that these children grow morally and physically healthy. And who should take care of this? Our teachers, our community. They are obliged to educate all children to live by principles, to persuade them and to make them courageous enough to take off their crosses in spite of the believers.

Is it difficult to achieve? No doubt about it. What is needed is not days or weeks, not one or another sensational measure; rather, persistent, day-by-day work of the teachers, and a sensitive, benevolent attitude of the community is of utmost importance.

Some people, upon reading these lines, may justly note: well, all this advice is too general. Yes, that's how it is. It is so because the work of an atheist means reaching human minds, and his way is usually different in each case, depending upon the individual who needs his advice and his cordial sympathy.

Naturally, the way of the teacher-atheist of Iaroslavl, in reaching the minds of the children of the servant of God will be quite different from that of the Byelorussian physician, Petr Stepanovich Poleiko of the village of Khoino in Polissia. He, Petr Stepanovich, is convinced that the main thing in the fight against superstition is not crowded lectures or some other large-scale program, but first of all intimate talks with people in which there may be quarrels, disputes and, above all, explanations by the physician-atheist. This is why Petr Stepanovich does not need any club hall or a colored poster announcing his lecture; he goes into every house and is prepared to explain for hours the harmfulness of superstitions, sorcery and adherence to old, obsolete customs.

Again, the lecture group of the village of Nizovka, Ardatovskii Region, Mordovia, has its own way to the minds of the audience. The leader of the group, A. Lenin, reports to our editor how thoroughly they prepare for every lecture, talk with a family or even for a conversation with any individual.

Letters . . . letters . . . There are many of them in our mail to the editor and, among them, there are many that tell about the work of village atheists. They are different letters, but they usually show a unity in one thing: a sincere gratitude to people who know how to fight against religious dope.

O. Tonkikh

1966

Source: *Doshkolnoe Vospitanie* (Pre-School Education), No. 3, March 1966, pp. 91—95

31

The Road Without God Is Wider

Children are born to be happy

We received many letters in reference to the article "This Should Never Be Forgotten." The readers ask: "What facts, proving the evil of religion, can be mentioned in the talks with parents; what should be suggested as reading material on atheism; what is the best way to separate children from the influence of religion?" But *they also ask such questions as: "Why is it that the atheists oppose religion with such ardor, what wrong did it cause to people and why is it dangerous to children?"* After all, in our times one cannot find religious people even with a lamp on a bright day *(Doshkolnoe Vospitanie,* No. 7, 1963).

As a member of the City Council I am the Chairman of the permanent Committee which controls the execution of the laws concerning [religious] cults, and, therefore, I can state with authority that many people are under the influence of religion and that religion continues its search for new souls. Acting either gradually or pushing their way through, the church people are trying to use every possible opportunity to strengthen their position. In their struggle for the believers, they generously use sweet words about love of your neighbors, and they do not hesitate to apply kindness or threat, money or violence.

Here is an example: In May 1965 I was present at the meeting of the old-rite church *Dvadtsiatka* [group of twenty]. There was under discussion the review of the report on the misappropriation of 4,000 rubles by the Treasurer of the congregation, S. I. Orlov, and other members. *In the church, where little lights were burning in front of the icons and the shine of flickering candlelight played on the faces of the "saints,"* the members of the *Dvadtsiatka* sect had nearly started a fight accusing each other of fraud (there were talks about cheating in the candle business, profiteering from selling crosses, etc.).

And what hatred and malice they showed in respect to one member of our Committee for the only reason that he had read the complaints of the believers at the Executive Committee! They threatened to "annihilate him from the face of the Earth."

Here is their love toward their neighbor and following "God's Laws": "do not steal, do not kill!"

The membership of this sect of old-rite *Dvadtsiatka* basically consists of people aged fifty and over (over seventy per cent). In its majority the sect consists of women (ninety per cent). Many of them did not attend church before their retirement age but then, after reaching old age, started regular attendance. *Some of them are afflicted with religious fanaticism to such an extent that they start exerting influence upon the members of their families, especially on the youth and children.*

All this compels us definitely to improve the atheist education. The workers of the kindergarten should attempt to know better every family so that they be able, in time, to prove helpful to the parents and children.

One should open the young parents' eyes concerning the baptism of the babies: after all, during the immersion of the baby into the water, a sudden death can occur if water gets into the respiratory tract.

Physicians of the epidemic centers have discovered that during the baptism and Communion even the most basic rules of sanitation and hygiene are neglected: the babies are bathed all in the same water in turn without it being disinfected; neither is the spoon disinfected by which the priest distributes "the blood and body of God" to the communicants.

At our pedagogical consultations and at our group or general meeings, there is always this one item of the order of the day: the atheistic education of the children and antireligious propaganda among the parents.

In addition to "radio lessons" conducted by the city, at which our educators and some parents appear with lectures and talks, we arrange similar programs in the kindergartens. The parents can receive counsel, hear a lecture or read books. We also organize the so-called home lessons. For this purpose, we prepare materials on atheism and give them to families. Also, we attend movies or theaters in groups and then discuss what we saw. For example, the educator V. V. Blagoderova saw, together with the parents, the motion pictures *Everything Remains With People*, and S. V. Boikova and N. N. Smirnova—the picture *The Miraculous One*. Then they exchanged their views.

We also devoted to the struggle against the religious ideology our "talking magazine for parents" which started at the club of the Railroad men and then continued at our kindergarten. The magazine had such articles as "Medicine, Religion and Witchcraft," "Science and Superstitions," "On Space Flights," etc.

Our active educators continue to increase their knowledge. It cannot be otherwise, because the parents often ask questions which have to be answered. We collect newspaper articles on interesting topics, we have assembled a library on atheism, have prepared a list of literature recommended for parents, etc. Among them are, e.g., A. Chekhov, *Kanitel, On the Eve of Fasting, The Secret;* A. Kuprin, *Olesia, Anafema;* A. Serafimovich, *The Holy Place (?), The Miracle, The Sacrament of Communion;* M. Gorkii, *Pamphlets, The Honeymoon, The Pogroms;* V. Tendriakov, *The Miraculous One, Omuta;* M. Twain, *A Letter to an Angel, Captain Stromfield's Visit to Heaven;* and E. Ozheshko, *The Witch.*

The church uses many popular holidays, customs and rites for its purposes; by attributing to them religious forms and mystical character, it created its own special religious rites, ceremonies and holidays. In opposition, we present our own customs and holidays, e.g. "Winter Tale," "Russian Birch," "Happy Childhood," and we celebrate in the kindergarten birthdays of the children.

Such a holiday was, e.g. the performance of "Happy Childhood" celebrated on June 1st, the "Day of Care of Children." Children, dressed for the occasion, marched to Lenin's monument and to the Obelisk of the Dead Soldiers. They placed a great number of fresh flowers at the foot of these monuments.

In the alleys of the park—there was laughter, games, dances. After that the children went by busses to the House of Culture to see the puppet theater. In the evening they enjoyed fireworks.

Once a month (on the 14th) we, in the kindergarten, celebrate children's birthdays. On this day children and teachers exchange gifts and also parents bring their gifts to the kindergarten.

We all gather in the hall: we offer our gifts and congratulations and, following a half-hour concert, we take seats at the tables which are decorated with flowers and on which are placed cookies, cakes and candies. If the birthday is celebrated in the spring or fall, the parents plant a tree in the garden of the kindergarten. We have many such trees, especially in the groups of the teachers G. V. Shankovaia and A. I. Vorobiovaia.

We pay a lot of attention to the upbringing in the spirit of Communist morality. The city-organized parent-teacher meeting was devoted to this purpose, and the question how to improve the atheistic education in schools and kindergartens was discussed.

All this we can do only together with the families.

M. Skei
Supervisor of the Kindergarten at Rzhev

OUR PASSIVENESS SUPPORTS RELIGION

My parents were poor peasants. *My father firmly believed in God and read the Bible every day. This book lay on the table like a sacred thing. In the mornings he would make us—his six children—kneel in front of the icons, kneel to the right beside us and read the prayers which we were supposed to repeat after him.*

Both our father and mother knew how to sing nicely. *While sewing clothing, preparing hemp for weaving linen or doing some other work, they would sing religious songs and we, the children, liked their singing so much that, involuntarily, we learned them. When we grew older we started to sing with them.*

When I was ten years old, my father told me to join the church choir. So I walked four to five kilometers [about three miles] to the village where the church was located. Not only me: the greater part of the church choir consisted of inhabitants of our village. The sexton would come to our village for rehearsals. In the evenings we would gather for rehearsals in one of our people's houses (in turns); next day the sexton would leave.

My turn came. Mother became restless: "What should I

offer the sexton to eat? I'll run over to Marusia to find out what they gave him: after all, it's Lent now."

We would eat cooked or baked potatoes, sour cabbage and cucumbers.

When mother returned from cousin Marusia, she had a piece of bacon, rolls, a bottle of milk and some ten eggs. For all this one had to work two days with the thrasher.

The rehearsal ended, the choir members left. Mother heated the stove, fried the eggs with bacon and put them on the table along with a glass of milk. She also placed some vodka on the table. But we, as usual, received baked potatoes, cabbage, cucumbers and dark bread.

The smell from the fried eggs and bacon spread all over the room and made our mouths water profusely.

"If we could just taste a little of the bacon," my brother said. "But it would be a sin. You would get a swelling like an egg on your head for eating fat things. This is what mother taught us," I replied, "and during the Lent, at that, just before Easter."

So we stupid ones waited for the morning to see the swelling on the sexton's head from the eggs, milk and bacon. But he got up as if nothing had happened, happily patting his belly. He ate the same for breakfast and departed.

We all turned to mother with question after question. But she, shocked and puzzled, just stood in front of the icons, crossed herself and said: "Forgive me, O God!"

For us, the children, this was the end of our believing in God. So it was for our mother. We felt that she performed the Easter rites only for the appearance's sake, and she hardly attended church. I participated in the church choir until I got married. I went there not because I believed in God, but there was nowhere to go.

I saw the fraud even more when I observed the priests dividing their income and quarreling with each other.

And when my mother fell sick and felt that she might die soon, she told me: "Watch out, don't let this liar priest bury me."

Even now *there are people in our country who let their children grow up as believers*. Our indifference, our passiveness plays a major role in this.

One should not let it happen that the children remain under the influence of the believers. And we, the workers of kindergartens, still do little to prevent this.

Only when children come to the kindergarten with a cross or an Easter egg, or when they do not come at all because they go to church with their grandmothers, we start to act and we act quietly in order not to hurt the feelings of the parents or children and so that other children in the group do not notice anything. What is needed is a persistent, planned atheistic work. This is the only way to stop the influence of religion upon the children.

M. Dobrenia,
Teacher at Sumy

THE EASTER EGG

Children crowded around Kola. There was a colored egg in the boy's hand. All watched the egg attentively and many tried to touch it.

Seeing me, the children cried:

"Look what a pretty egg Kola has!"

"Yes, it is pretty," I agreed. I could not say that it was not pretty, because it would not be true.

"It was Easter yesterday," Kola explained seriously, then he added: "We have many like this one."

"I ate the Easter bread *(pashka)* and such an egg yesterday on a visit," Tania said. "It was very, very good."

"And I think that this egg is like any other, quite ordinary," I remarked. The children listened. "It was lucky that nothing happened to Tania and Kola; after all, the color is poisonous, so they could have got sick."

"Why, then, do they color the eggs?" one of the children asked. Then I decided to tell the children about this religious holiday.

"It was long, long ago. At that time people did not know why the rain or the snow comes down, why the wind blows, the thunder cracks, the lightning strikes.... They then invented God and said that it was He that did all this. The reason for this was that people did not know much. But now, even you know well how the rain starts."

"There were no physicians at that time. People got sick and there was nobody to cure them; so many died. And, again, people believed that it was God that sent death, and He did it to bad people. But good people died too. It was believed that God lived in heaven above. But what do you think is there above us in the sky?" [Translator's note: the same term, *nebo,* means heaven or sky in Russian.]

"Clouds."

"Right. And above the clouds?"

"Cosmos. The airless space!"

The children started talking about the cosmonauts, about Aleksei Leonov who left the space craft and stepped out into space.

"The people assumed that God lived in heaven the way we live on earth. In order to gain His favors, everybody tried to serve Him something tasty: they baked cakes, cookies and colored eggs to make them look nice . . . Yet God would not come to take these things. How could He come? But He does not exist. Then people ate everything themselves. Even nowadays some uneducated people still think, in that old way, that God lives in heaven, and continue to color eggs for Him in order to eat them afterwards."

The children laughed gaily and looked at Tania. The girl turned, red-faced.

One year passed. Ola's mother, who came to the kindergarten to pick up her daughter, told me that their grandmother had suddenly announced:

"I have bought eggs. Easter is near."

Upon hearing this, Ola started enlightening her grandmother. We all listened. Then Ola asked:

"Now, Grandma, do you believe that there is no God?"

Who knows what the grandmother was thinking, but she told her granddaughter:

"Yes, I believe, I believe."

Then Ola kissed her grandmother on both her cheeks.

S. Zhilak
City of Minsk

IT IS POOR HELP FROM WITCH DOCTOR AND GOD

No persuasion or promises would help: the married couple would not be reconciled—the husband left Elizaveta Tsegelniuk. Now, this worker of Kindergarten No. 19 in Petrozavodsk decided to turn for outside help. She heard from somebody that there lived in the city a sorceress who could do everything: to return the loved one and to foretell trouble.

The woman went to the address given to her on Volodarskogo Street. The sorceress met the new customer in a very friendly way. She recognized at once that she did not come empty handed.

The seance of witchcraft lasted quite a while. It included questions and secret whispering over some liquid which the deserted "queen of hearts" was supposed to drink in one gulp. Elizaveta returned home full of hopes. After all, the sorceress had promised her that her husband would surely return to her and even love her more than before. She even fixed the exact date of this return: November 10th.

On that day Elizaveta sat by the window from early morning till late at night, but in vain; the husband did not come back. The woman went to the sorceress with complaints. "Wait," the latter told her again, "be patient. Others wait much longer." She sat down on a stool, put a pail with water in front of her and started gazing into it.

"I see it quite clearly, your loved one will come back."

So Elizaveta started waiting.

And the sorceress did not waste time: she cured not only the soul but also the body; she charmed illnesses away.

She was particularly eager to cure children. She knew that parents would give everything to make the child well again. The sorceress had a firm fee for everything: for example—the price of charming away of hernia in a boy was three rubles or a cake.

Most of all, the sorceress is visited by believing parents or members of families who bring up children. They think that shots and bitter medicines applied by the doctors are cruel. On the other hand, a sorcerer is kind, merciful. . . . His words are sweet and the liquids [sweetened] with honey. He would pray some and then give the needy one holy water or some herbs to drink. . . .

Using the limitless confidence of a child who trusts that the parents wish him well, the adults, because of their ignorance, cause damage to their children.

At Davlekanov, Kola Fedaev fell sick. His condition grew increasingly worse. When the boy lost consciousness the parents lost their heads. But the local sorceress, Shvedova, came to their help. She started to pray, to charm the sickness away, and forbade the calling of a physician: he would interfere with "the word."

When medical help was called for, anyhow, the boy was in a very serious condition. The physicians could hardly save him.

Some people, especially in remote places, far away from cultural centers, still blindly trust the sorcerers who, they believe, are endowed with abilities given to them by some sacred power and, therefore, can cure all illnesses.

In the village of Kovarzino of the Vologodskaia Oblast [Province], a funny thing happened. A woman had a heart condition and turned to a doctor who prescribed a drug. She took it for a long period of time, but did not feel any better. The woman was discouraged.

Then the pious women advised: "You should go and see Mazikha. She has a magic word and special water for everything. Mazikha will help you for sure."

The woman asked her acquaintance, a nurse working in the local hospital, to go to Mazikha. The nurse could not refuse the request of a sick friend, but at the same time, could not very well go to the sorcerer: after all, she was a medical employee. The whole village would laugh at her. But she found a way out. She went to the village store, bought a bottle of Vermouth wine, removed the label and the sealing wax and brought the bottle to the sick one.

"Take one small glass of it before dinner, Mazikha said to tell you."

This "charmed medicine" was the woman's last hope. She took it for one week and felt much better. She regained her good mood and went to work.

Only then her friend confessed to her the truth. And it was not the contents of the bottle that helped the woman, but rather the belief that she would get well.

Unfortunately, it is not always that the stories connected with the sorcerers end in a comical way. More often they bring about serious effects and tragic solutions.

Nurlan, the son of Gazimshan Khusainov, a worker of the Pritobolskii sovkhoz in the Kustanaiskii Region, underwent circumcision. The boy started bleeding. The parents called a sorcerer. He came and started his charms, reciting some words. Naturally it would not help. The seven-year-old boy passed away.

And here is what happened in Tadzhikistan. Akmoldzhan Babadzhanov was growing strong and happy. Suddenly he fell sick. The right thing to do was to take him to the hospital where the physicians would restore him to health in a few days. But his parents went to the neighboring village to see the "healer" Muin. The first thing he did was to demand a large sum of money and only after that he started his healing procedure from a distance, by prayers. The condition of the sick boy did not improve. The Muin went to see the sick boy at his home. He looked at his mouth, into his eyes, tried the weak muscles and eventually declared:

"He has too much blood. He should be kept for ten days without food."

The boy was locked up in a shed. He cried for a long time, but nobody would care to look after him. After ten days Muin appeared, examined the sick boy and said:

"Everything goes the way it should." With an old razor, he cut the vein on Akmoldzhan's arm. He let out a great deal of blood and, having said his prayers, dressed the wound with a dirty rag, took as his fee a lamb and a great deal of things, and left for home.

After a few days the boy died from infection. It was only the interference of authorities that prevented other fatalities.

Such are the sorcerers. They are ignorant, half-literate people, adventurers and charlatans. Upon a closer look at the facts of "healing" practices of these people, it seems incredible that these "healers" could be trusted: in cases of skin inflammation, they apply dirty wool, green dirt [moss?], tobacco, etc.; in cases of burns and frostbites, they apply fresh poultry dung; they cure dislocation with charming or massaging with wheel grease. For their practice they use dog's dung, human urine, spiders, woodlice, black roaches and ground glass. They often apply poisonous matters, sublimate, mercury or arsenic without understanding their effects on human organism and having no idea of dosage.

"All sicknesses come from God," the religion teaches. "He is sending them to people for their sins." Apparently, they are caused by evil spirits which penetrate into the body of a man; so in order to heal him those spirits must be chased out. For this purpose it is necessary to carry the "holy cross," to pray, drink water which had been blessed in church or taken from "holy" wells. The belief in the miraculous powers of the cross, the prayers, the "holy" water, etc. originates the belief in the powers of the sorcerers and healers. Thus, religion does not repudiate socery because both are then results of ignorance and the erring of man.

In Tsarist Russia, when the Orthodox Church, through its beliefs and teachings, served the absolutism and dominated the minds of people, the sorcery flourished. At that time, e.g., they maintained that malaria was the deed of the twelve bad daughters of King Herod. Even its name *likhoradka* apparently originated from *Likhoi* (the bad one) as the evil spirit was called.

The sorcerers assumed that, if the sick person suffered from shivering, it was the virgins *Ledea* and *Triasea* that got hold of him. If fever started in the sick person, it was the virgin *Ognea;* if his bones were aching or he felt pressure, the virgins *Lomea* and *Gnetea* were responsible. [Translator's note: the names of the virgins have roots which convey the meaning of the particular afflictions in Russian.] Accordingly, the "proper" treatment was prescribed.

In our country, best conditions for the fight against illnesses have been created. The multitude of hospitals, free medical assistance, etc., have considerably undermined the influence of religion and, consequently, of sorcery. However, even in our times sorcerers can be found. They use the backwardness of the people and their belief in God and in supernatural forces.

The church leaders and sectarians also use smartly the superstitions and prejudices. Relying on them, they seek to increase the number of their flock and to raise their authority. Here is what the former church servant, E. Doluman, tells us:

"Once, during the Holy Communion, one of the women in the church started to holler in a low voice:

" 'Oh, oh! Don't do that, I am going to leave her! Oooh!'

" 'She is possessed, possessed,' people whispered.

"Two strong men came up to the woman and tried to hold her. The woman struggled. Finally, she calmed down and said in a quiet voice:

" 'I do want to receive Holy Communion. . . . It is the evil spirit inside me that cries. . . .'

"Then she hollered again at the top of her voice. The possessed was given Communion by force and only then she quieted down.

"The happening with the possessed woman strengthened my belief in the power of the Holy Communion. However, when three weeks later, the same woman appeared in the church, again in the company of the same two strong men, I decided to test her. I approached the woman and said firmly:

" 'If the evil spirit starts shouting again, I am going to call the ambulance to take you to the madhouse.'

" 'You Antichrist,' the "possessed" woman replied angrily. 'And a seminarian at that! After all, I am shouting for the glory of God. Don't you understand?' "

In one of the religious sects, unexpectedly "brother" Anton Gotelaka fell sick. Rumors spread that he was crushed by a tree cut in the woods. The sectarian leaders would tell the people: "The poor man suffered an open fracture of both legs. Physicians could not help him. He has been bedridden for several months now. He might even pass away to go to the Kingdom of Heaven."

The sectarians decided to ask God to perform a miracle and to heal the sick man. And, sure enough, the "miracle" happened: as soon as they started the public prayers, Gotelaka got up from his bed and started walking in his room, without even limping.

"A miracle, a miracle!" the believers shouted.

Only later on, Gotelaka admitted that he was not sick at all. It was the sectarian leaders who suggested that he help to perform the "miracle."

Religious superstitions and prejudices are very harmful. They keep the sick ones from getting legitimate treatment. The sorcerers indoctrinate people by implanting in their minds the idea that they are completely dependent on the heavenly power, which, as we know, does not exist. Sick persons do not get medical aid in time and the sickness continues to develop, becomes chronic and brings about complications. Being caught in the dragnets of the sorcerers, the sick ones allow their illness to become incurable.

Not only physicians should fight against religion and sorcery but also masses of the population, including the workers of kindergartens. People who avoid medical aid should be instructed that it is only medicine that can ease their suffering.

Il. Okunev

Source: *Pravda Ukraini,* July 12, 1966, p. 4

32

They Received What They Deserved

From the Courtroom:

In the House of Culture of Shipbuilders at Sadovaia Street, a trial against the organizers of the sect of the *Piatidesiatniki* was in progress.

P. I. Zaichenko, V. I. Borbunevich and A. A. Iakimenko, who call themselves Christians of Evangelical Faith, were brought before the Court.

Their admissions and the testimony of witnesses depicted a gloomy picture of a truly wild fanaticism of the style of the Middle Ages.

The basic objective of the *Piatidesiatniki* is to keep Soviet people away from community life. These three defendants preached to old, young and quite minor people: "Do not read newspapers, do not attend movies or theaters, do not watch television programs, do not listen to the radio broadcast!" They harmed their "brothers" and "sisters," stupefied them, and brought upon them physical and moral trauma.

It was not by accident that one of the members of the sect, A. Reznichenko, after being "baptized by the Spirit" and after "talking in tongues" [*glossolalia*] was driven to a complete stupefaction and fell seriously ill. The fanatic [Mrs.] Ioanna Sinko exaggerated in praying to such an extent that she now suffers from epileptic seizures. In [Mrs.] Nina Halushchak, physicians found the symptoms of a serious affection of her central nervous system. During their praying sessions, the sectarians drove the girl pupil Liuda Ploshnik and the children Ira Pushkareva, Olef Lebedev and Vasia Ploshnik to a psychological derangement and a state of dead faint.

These and many other victims burden the conscience of the leaders of the sect of the *Piatidesiatniki* at Nikolaev. They destroyed the family of V. Voznenko, and brought to the brink of breakup the family of I. Sinko.

During all Court days the hall of the House of Culture

of the Shipbuilders was filled to capacity. Representatives of the collectives of the Kirov tailoring plant and of the Streetcar Management appeared before the Court. They demanded strict punishment of the wild fanatics. Also the workers of other enterprises, schools and agencies sent letters to the Court, expressing the same sentiments.

The Court passed a judgment which was met by the whole community of the city with sincere approval: Zaichenko, Borbunevich and Iakimenko were sentenced to five years in prison each.

Nikolaev
A. Magin

Source: *Sovetskaia Latviia*, February 9 (no year given)

33

Is Stepanov a Lost Man?

The meeting at the Repair and Construction Department of the Moscow Region of Riga was fully attended. It lasted about three and one-half hours. Many were not able to find seats and had to stand. Even those who usually keep quiet spoke up.

But let us tell the story from the beginning. At the Repair and Construction Department there is employed as a foreman Nikolai Stepanov. He enjoys a good reputation. His brigade fulfills its quota, receives premiums so that, it would seem, the managers should not wish anything else.

Nobody really knew who Stepanov was. Some time in the past, he was a preacher in the Russian Baptist Congregation at Riga. Then he was removed from this position. Having lost his comfortable position, *Stepanov formed his own Baptist group which often gathered in the apartments of the believers. In violation of the existing Laws concern-*

ing religious cults, Stepanov several times conducted religious services.

But this was not all. He visited several Baptist communities in the Republic and appeared before the believers. Stepanov visited Sigulda and Iaunelgava, Tukuma and Liepaia.

Now, talking about the improper deeds of this man, one would like to ask the Presbyters of the Baptist Congregations, Egle, Pelchers, Strelis and others, on what basis they placed their pulpits at the disposal of the preacher who had no right to preach?

But this is not yet all. Stepanov distributed among the believers booklets which contained crude lies about our way of life. In these booklets, which are bombastically called "Protest," Stepanov's fellow believers maintain that the believers in our country are subject to persecutions.

I can easily imagine how these "documents" are compiled. Someplace, two Baptist preachers must have met secretly, put a map on the wall and got to work. One, closing his eyes, pointed his finger at the map and, in such way, found the names of the localities: the other one decided what to write.

For example, the finger hit a place somewhere in Siberia.

"Tiumen," the Baptist called.

"Well, all right," the other continued. "Let's write that there was a trial against the believers at Tiumen. Go on."

"Kurgan."

"Fine. Let's say that the Baptist Congregation was liquidated at Kurgan. Proceed!"

"Dniepropetrovsk."

"We'll announce that there the believers were deprived of their living quarters."

In such a way, looking alternately at the map and at the ceiling, they continued in their "work." They included in the "Protest" a dozen or so of all kinds of Soviet towns. Who does not believe, let him go to Tiumen, Kurgan or another place to check. Surely, you would not go.

The authors of the "Protest" count on this fact. It is a known fact that, basically, people of little education, and politically uninformed constitute the vast majority of the believers. Some of them, reading such a "document" which, at that, they received from a former preacher, may in fact accept it as true.

In addition to all this, *Stepanov attempted to forward this lie abroad.*

When the improper dealings of the former Baptist preacher became known, the Workers gathered together in order to judge the behavior of the member of their collective.

Stepanov is given the floor. His speech is flowery, full of ambiguities, hints and obscure statements. He begins with references to Lenin, asserts his proletarian descent, assures that he never served in Hitler's Army, did not fire a single shot. Then he attempts to repudiate some facts. He is then asked questions. His answers are, e.g., like this:

Question: "Is it a fact that you went to Liepaia and distributed the 'Protests' to the believers?"

Answer: "Yes, I went there. But I know nothing about the distribution of 'Protests.' "

Question: "But when you went to Liepaia, were these papers with you?"

Answer: "Yes, they were."

Question: "Where did you deliver them?"

Answer: "I do not remember."

This is how the discussion goes on.

As we can see, the former "divine" father does not show a simple human sincerity in front of his fellow workers. Those gathered asked him to mention at least one fact concerning persecution of the believers in our country, but Stepanov does not know of any such facts.

"Here, too, we do not judge you because you are a believer, but because you violate Soviet laws," the economist A. Rabiner says. "The considerable majority of our people are atheists. But we do not consider the believers to be our enemies, because they are the same Soviet citizens as we are, and enjoy the same rights as us. All we require is that the priests fulfill the provisions of Law."

"You quoted Lenin," another says. "Well, it is then only fair to say, that Lenin himself was an ardent fighter against religious foolishness. It is Lenin who is credited with the slogan: 'Religion is a sort of spiritual raw brandy.' "

In the room applause is heard.

Stepanov was forced to hear many bitter but just words that evening. The workers, A. Kozlov, A. Tarasenko, and V. Kirilenko, retired people and former employees of the management, V. Tarabarin, V. Denisov and others, all said that our people would not allow anybody to violate Laws.

And still, the fellow workers expressed the hope that Stepanov was not yet a completely lost man, that he still might come to senses and change. The collective of the Department offers him such a chance.

When you think of this incident you involuntarily recall what L. F. Il'ichev said in his speech at the June Plenary Session of the Central Committee of the Communist Party of the Soviet Union: "It happens often in our midst that a man works nicely in his enterprise, but at home violates the rules of socialistic community life. Most of the time nobody cares about such a double life. This is why, at home, the survivals of the past, including religious prejudices, are particularly strong."

The incident at the Repair and Construction Department again proves this statement to be true. It discloses that, in its ideological work among the collective, the Party organization of the management does not reach every person.

The Central Committee of the Communist Party of the Soviet Union suggested that all local Party organizations, together with the Labor Unions and the *Komsomol,* should investigate the religious status in each collective. The Party organization of the Repair and Construction Department has a great deal to do in this respect. It is obvious that the comrades lack fighting spirit and the knowledge of how to oppose the ideological foe.

When Stepanov was given the floor, he took a lot of time trying to confuse those present and make foolish statements. And what happened? The Communists sat there and showed kindness to the demagogue who was in the possession of the rostrum. And only then a man stood up and said:

"Comrades, what is going on here? How long are we going to listen to all this jabber?"

For a long time Stepanov had one face at the enterprise where he worked and another one at his home. Now the former Baptist preacher showed to the collective (of his fellow workers) his true face.

Will he be able to learn a lesson from all that was said at the meeting?

Only time will tell.

(Signature illegible)

Source: *Izvestia*, June 5, 1966, p. 6; (complete text)

34

Prophets and Victims

Assignment at Reader's Request: 1966

At the very edge of Mtsensk, where the quiet little street called Sadovaya comes to an end, stands a shabby white house. Through its long-unwashed windows it peers ominously out at the shining, noisy traffic on the Moscow-Simferopol Highway. A crowd of enraged people can be seen beside that house nearly every day now. If the militia were not here, the incensed people probably would have torn that house from the face of the earth, so shaken were the minds and hearts of people by the tragedy recently played out in the house. Here a frenzied fanatic slaughtered her neighbor's child in broad daylight. Before the eyes of his father and mother.

Little Valery Mitichkin would have been three years old. The whole street knew this fair-haired boy. Everyone had long known his murderess, too, the sect member Maria Rykova. The neighbors had known and quarreled with her for many years. The wave of pain, anger and rage set off by the murder shook the whole of Sadovaya and then spread concentrically through all Mtsensk.

Izvestia sent me to Mtsensk at the request of the readers. I spoke to dozens of people, read the case records and visited the murderess in the Orel prison. The event is horrible, of course, and quite extraordinary. This is why we must tell about it now, without waiting for the investigation to be completed and for all the dark and gruesome aspects of the affair to come to light.

A wave of popular indignation shakes Mtsensk today. Wherever you go, people talk only about the tragedy on Sadovaya. The reports are swelled with all sorts of conjectures and fantastic surmises. Even in Tula and Orel I had heard utterly exaggerated versions of the tragedy. Rumors had even seeped in about sect terrorism.

Unfortunately, no one but the militia did any explanatory work in Mtsensk at the time, so the militia has had to combat rumors as well as protect Mtsensk sect members from spontaneous violence.

No sooner had I appeared at the ill-starred house than two women approached me, then two more, then several men, and soon the street was filled with an enraged crowd. People out-shouted one another:

"We wrote about that Rykova hornets' nest three years ago!"

"Maria wouldn't leave us alone!"

"She kept frightening our children."

"She kept trying to get everyone into her sect."

"The law should have been turned on these parasites long ago!"

"They eat Soviet bread, but trample on Soviet laws!"

I never thought I would ever have to act as a defender of Baptists. But this is just what I had to do. As I parried a storm of reproaches, angry questions and quick-tempered appeals for rash actions, I regretted that Comrade Parkhomenko, the Secretary of the Mtsensk Party Committee, was not in my place. No doubt he could have given a fuller answer to the chief and alas just accusation: Why hadn't the municipal organizations listened to the voice of the public in time?

The angry people around me were not vicious people. I answered their questions, objected, agreed and argued—and our talk, which had begun stormily, ended on a calm note.

Why had the people's wrath descended not only on the murderess and her kin but also on all sect members? Why did the indignant people so persistently link Maria Rykova's crime with her faith?

The murderess was in prison when I saw her. She was a strong, broad-shouldered woman with powerful arms and with coarse features set in a dull, stubborn expression. She answered my questions willingly, remembering perfectly well all the details, names and events. She spoke calmly of her crime.

Here is how Maria Rykova came to be religious. She grew up with her grandmother, who sedulously instilled in her a faith in God ("I'm teaching her to be good, not bad"). Then Auntie Katya turned up; she convinced the girl that the faith of the Church was not the "true" one and led her off to Jehovah's Witnesses. But Maria did not like the Witnesses, for some reason, and did not belong to any sect for a while. Unfortunately there was at that time no wise and experienced person at her side. Instead, Auntie Tanya turned up and drew her into a community of Evangelical Christian Baptists. But the seeds planted by the Jehovah's Witnesses evidently had struck root. No sooner did dissenters appear in the Baptist community than Maria joined them.

The residents of the street where the child was brutally murdered did not know about all these sects and the distinctions between them. They saw only that the tragedy had occurred on religious grounds and knew that the murder had been attended by features resembling some sort of ritual. For instance, Rykova had dressed the boy in a clean, specially prepared baby's vest before killing him. They knew that the murderess was a Baptist and they blamed all sect members indiscriminately.

It goes against my grain to defend Baptists. Poisoning human souls with religious opiates is always fraught with dangerous consequences, no matter how innocuously this is done! Frequently the Baptist plough the souls of their brethren in Christ, and others—barbarously fanatical sects —sow this well-prepared soil.

Nonetheless, one must be objective. Ritual murder is alien to the convictions and faith of Baptists; otherwise this sect would have been forbidden by law. Only lack of information on the subject and the poor organization of explanatory work in Mtsensk can account for the panicky rumors sweeping the city from end to end: "The Baptists will slaughter our children," and hence the conclusion: "Drive out the Baptists!"

Still, there are people walking about who deserve the full fury of that wrath. They are not many, only a few. Hiding from the Law and the people, they do their shady work in secret. Their tentacles reached out even to this place, to the edge of Mtsensk.

For some time now, certain petitioners have been turning up in the waiting rooms of offices in the provinces, the republics and even the capital. They call themselves Baptists, but hasten to stress that the present Baptist Church "does not conform to the teachings of Christ" and that they have dissented with it.

These petitioners behave defiantly, at times clearly provoking rows. The petitions they present to the officials contain illegal demands (not requests, but demands!) formulated in two points:

First: That their so-called "organizational committee" be charged with convoking an all-Union Baptists' congress that would remove the present leadership of the community and put in its place the leadership of the organizational committee. Second: "That interference by school and State in the upbringing of the believers' children be discontinued."

Such was the petition which they addressed to the Council for Religious Affairs and other official agencies. Everywhere, it was patiently explained to them that convoking a congress of believers was an internal affair of the religious community itself, since the Church is separate from the State in our country. If State bodies were to tell the present leadership of the Union of Evangelical Christian Baptists to convoke a congress, they would be breaking the law; and instructions on which leaders to remove and whom to replace them with would be all the more unlawful.

It was also explained to them that we have a law on universal education and that every child must receive a secular education, regardless of his parents' convictions.

When the more literate of the petitioners were asked why they are dissatisfied with the leadership of the Baptist community, they reply approximately as follows: "We recognize only divine law, while the present leadership of the Baptist Church recognizes earthly laws as well."

So this turns out to be the essence of the matter. The people behind the petitioners do not want to recognize the Laws of the Soviet State, nor to reckon with the fact that the sect members are not only believers but also Soviet citizens. Our laws protect the rights of believers but also Soviet citizens. Our laws protect the rights of believers and their religious liberty. The laws, however, oblige believers, as well as atheists, to do their civic duty as defined by the U.S.S.R. Constitution and to obey Soviet Laws. The leaders of the "organizational committee" are essentially opposed to the law. There are some laws which they accept, however: they draw their pensions punctually, and they willingly avail themselves of paid vacations and other benefits of our society, the established order of which they oppose.

They admonish their petitioners to pursue their illegal

demands by all conceivable means, even by raising an uproar. They instill in them the idea that this means "fighting for the true faith," for the petitioners as a rule have only a feeble understanding of the subtleties in the petitions. They are simply drilled to "stand up for the faith" to "suffer" for it. And it is for this that they come to the province centers and the capital.

Recently I had occasion to talk to two such petitioners. What is it that they are advocating so tenaciously?

Anna Fyodorovna Istratova, fifty-two years old and single, is a charwoman at a Tula factory. Obeying an order from her sect leaders, she dropped her job and set off with a petition. She had only the vaguest notion of the contents of the petition. "I am petitioning so that the other, the registered Baptists, won't persecute us, for there is no truth in them."

Akim Ivanovich Bobylev (sixty-two years old, he collects a respectable pension) came from Bryansk Province (presumably to Moscow) fully convinced that he was soliciting permission to register his congregation with the representative of the Council for Religious Affairs. He was very surprised when it turned out that he was soliciting exactly the opposite—the abrogation of the legal status of sects.

Behind the backs of these generally backward and unscrupulously deceived people stands the adventurist group of the so-called "organizational committee," driving headlong for power over the Baptist community and its treasury. The group is headed by Gennady Kryuchkov and Georgy Vins; it is they who fit out the petitioners and direct them from hideouts, urging them to stand up almost "in the name of the people." Actually, they have no right to speak even on behalf of the Baptist community, for they have been able to deceive and carry with them less than a twentieth of all the Baptists.

Defeated inside the community, the "organizational committee" promoted seething underground activity. It recruited adherents through deception and incited them to ever more brazen and provocative acts. Now it needs "victims of persecution" and "martyrs of the faith" to rekindle the believers' cooling interest.

It was with such Baptists that Maria Rykova was associated for the past two or three years. It was they who taught her to disobey secular Laws. It was they who fanned her fanaticism and her readiness to "defend the faith of Christ" by any conceivable means.

A marked change in Rykova's behavior coincided with the period of intensive activity by the "organizational committee" adherents. Until then she had prayed fervently at the secret meetings of her sect, openly advocated her views and proselytized whoever she could for the sect. She even promised a cow to little Valery's mother, Nina Mitichkina.

All this attracted no particular attention from the general public. Her neighbors, true enough, had demanded that local organizations look into what was going on in her family and find out at the same time what they lived on. It was a big family with a small income, yet they had bought a motorcycle, then a motorscooter and now were trying to buy a car. But these warning signals went unheeded.

Then came March. The sect intensified its propaganda to resist Soviet Laws, and Maria received underground literature calling for a struggle against "secular Laws" and for obedience to "divine law." Found in her home during the search that followed the murder were several issues of the illegal "Brethren's Leaflet" (the latest was the April issue) and the notorious "address to All Mothers in Registered and Unregistered Congregations of the Evangelical Baptist Faith in the U.S.S.R." This contained the summons: "Unite our efforts in prayer to God to dedicate to his service our children's lives from the cradle." It also carried the appeal: "Save our children from the influence of the world."

We do not know how these documents were interpreted to Maria Rykova, by her secret spiritual father, a certain Zamaruyev, and by visiting "spreaders of the faith." One can guess, however, that they were not sparing of appeals to action.

When Maria's oldest son, Vanya, was admitted to the Young Pioneers in April, Maria tore off his kerchief and forbade Lyuba, who was in the first grade, to wear the star of the Young Octoberists (an organization of children younger than the Pioneers). Then she went to school and declared that her children were believers and were not to be admitted to the Young Pioneers and Young Octoberists.

Maria's mother, Anastasia Vasilyevna, was troubled about her grandchildren's lives; she brought Vanya another kerchief and urged her daughter not to cripple the children's souls. Maria did not give in, and repulsed her mother. Thereupon Anastasia Vasilyevna began to petition to have her daughter deprived of maternal rights and her children taken from her! This warning signal too was ignored.

On Sunday, May 22, Maria's husband took her to a secret prayer meeting by motorcycle. When she returned she was excited. We do not know what was said at that meeting. Only one document bearing that date has been preserved, Rykova's draft of a statement that her son was allegedly being persecuted at school for his religion. On the same day Maria learned from her husband that he had taken their neighbors by motorcycle to pick a cow for purchase, and that the neighbors had already received a 300-ruble loan from the State (for the purchase of the cow). This meant that they had decided to do without her draft.

Early on the morning of May 23 Maria called Nina from her house and told her that unless she returned the loan at once, she would pay dearly for it. She also warned her that there was a great secret behind her words. Nina and her husband thought it over and decided that perhaps a monetary reform was in the offing. Her husband took the money and went to work at the factory. His wife left the house an hour later. On her way out she was stopped by Rykova at the gate: "Why take little Valery along with you? Leave him with us." The mother left him in Rykova's care, as she had done many times before. At the factory Nina learned that Maria had already been there to ask the bookkeeper whether the loan had been returned. The mother hastened back. Maria refused to open the door to her, and said through the window that she would not return the son until she received a certificate saying that the money had been returned. Maria now ran to her husband, who came rushing home to demand his son. The house was carefully locked from the inside. Maria's own children had been sent away somewhere. Through the window Rykova showed him a knife and declared that unless he brought the certificate little Valery would live only until two o'clock.

Little Valery's terrified parents ran for the militia. In a few minutes a militia car arrived on the scene, having picked up Rykova's husband on the way. The husband's negotiations with his wife came to nothing. Nina looked through the window and went into hysterics. Maria had the weeping child, dressed in a pink vest, squeezed between her knees. She held a knife in her hand.

All hurled themselves against the window and door and broke into the house. But it was too late.

It is hard to imagine that a person of sound mind would resort to such a terrible act. But even if Rykova suffered a mental breakdown, isn't the cause obvious?

Whatever the experts may say and whatever the Court may decide, the death of Valery Mitichkin is on your consciences, Gennady Kryuchkov and Georgy Vins! It was you in your hideouts who kindled the evil passions in your followers' souls, you who sent the petitioners you had duped to "suffer for the faith," though you yourselves prefer to hide behind their backs.

Prophets of evil, you sow nothing but evil, though you hold forth about kindliness and love of one's neighbor. In what a sinister light your basic thesis suddenly appears, the thesis you have been drumming into your flock: "Do not submit to earthly law, submit to God's laws!" Who can foresee what monstrous shape this thesis may take in the inflamed mind of some semiliterate fanatic or other, now leafing through Holy Writ to get God's guidance on how he can best "champion" the faith.

Before I left Mtsensk, Aleksandr Petrovich Buzanov, Party organizer of a shop at the Nonferrous Metals Recovery Plant, looked me up at my hotel. He had come to ask me to deliver a talk in the shop and explain what it was all about.

"All I hear people say is: 'Why don't you suppress the Baptists? Why don't you exile them?' And I'm not in the know——"

I could not deliver that talk, but I put the assiduous Party organizer "in the know" to the best of my ability. After that, all the way back to Moscow, I pondered the question eternally asked by newspapers on such occasions: "Citizens, where were you?" The Mtsensk tragedy highlighted a strange and unforgettable inertia on the part of local organizations and the public. No conclusions were drawn, no lessons learned. Even the agitators were not called together in time, were not told about what had happened, were not assigned to where passions now are seething. And the Deputies to the City Soviet have not gone into their constituencies to carry to the voters the message that is needed at this moment.

A strange serenity. And dangerous.

Mtsensk
N. Shtanko

1967

Source: *Sovetskaia Belorussiia*, August 15, 1967

35

Extract from
"The Brutal Hypocrites"

A group of *ignorant fanatics from the Utevsk Baptist Evangelical Christian Church have woven their nest in the area. The praying hypocrites recognize only their "holy books,"* which are printed in America and England. These overseas businessmen are not wasting their efforts; their aims are obvious. By taking advantage of our religious freedom, *they are bringing into our country the germs of their rotten imperialist ideology.*

The most insolent of the Baptist pastors, in an outburst of disapproval of the Soviet Laws, declared themselves dissenters.

They are determined to convert the population and to establish the rule of *the "evangelical ideology" over the land; to introduce religious instruction of the children and the abolishment of antireligious propaganda. They begin to frighten the believers with fear of the "Great Judgment of God,"* urging all, "each personally," to earn their salvation by active recruitment and winning others to Christ.

The believers from Utevsk were the first to join the dissenters' movement. *Their pastor, F. Kopenkov, initiated the move. The hypocrites from Utevsk refused to recognize revolutionary holidays,* attend movies or watch television. They also refused to read "worldly" books, magazines and newspapers. *Their radio receivers were always tuned to foreign "soul-saving" radio broadcasts.*

Pastor F. Kopenkov, in his sermons, urged his fellow believers, whose minds were saturated with religious deception, to educate their children in religion; to invite members of their families and friends to join the church. Because of these illegal activities, Pastor F. Kopenkov was fined. This resentful fanatic then *organized public processions of believers. They sang psalms, almost driving themselves into a frenzy. Then the pastor urged the fanatics' parents to undertake new efforts to infect their children with religion and to draw them away from the influence of the schools. This was to prepare them for joining the Church. For this flagrant violation of the laws, Pastor F. Kopenkov was imprisoned.*

1968

Source: *Sovetskaia Rossiia* (Soviet Russia), Moscow, January 13, 1968, p. 4

36

Once Upon a Time There Was a Little Girl . . .

A letter received by the editor cannot be read dispassionately.

"... I strongly request that a thorough examination be made of my situation and the fate of my daughter Tanya. . . . I ask for help in blocking her path into religion and in condemning her grandmother and everyone who is helping to cripple the life of the child. . . ."

Vladimir Ovchinnikov
Khabarovsk

... There once was a little girl named Tanya. A short girl. With light-colored hair. Tanya had a mama and a papa. They had married before Papa's term of service in the army. And when Papa came back home he no longer lived with Tanya's mama. . . .

"I get the picture," thinks the reader. "A family drama. . . . Unfortunate children . . ."

Don't rush to the conclusion, Comrade. Everything here is vastly more involved. In addition, don't rush to condemn Tanya's father harshly, and by the way, Tanya's mother. The mother because she is no longer with us. She caught a cold. She took ill. In March this year she died. As for Papa . . .

I have purposely skipped over the middle of this sad story and have begun at the end. Now Tanya is eight. She is in the second grade of one of the Khabarovsk schools and is under the observation of a neuropathologist and a therapist. The little girl has a serious nervous affliction. Weakened cardiac activity. Incipient rheumocarditis.

And all this, I repeat, at eight years of age.

Yes, a family mess, and the mother's death of course could not but affect the health of little Tanya. But fairly recently, a much more weighty cause was uncovered, in

fact, in a Court trial. And right here we must turn back to
the deliberately skipped middle of the story.

Even during the lifetime of the mother, who, following a
divorce, received money from her ex-husband for child
support, Tanya was handed over for upbringing to the
home of a grandmother living in the settlement of Sita,
seventy kilometers from Khabarovsk.

Once, the grandmother, Evdokiya Afanas'yevna Zabavina, dressed the girl in her best clothes and took her
somewhere. It was on a Sunday. Autumn was still compet-
ing with the onset of winter. The chill tweaked Tanya's
cheeks. Grandmother led her to the home of the Baptist
Chernolevskiy, where many people had already come together. And then it began!

People sang, went through strange motions and entered
into ecstasy that was meaningless and strange to the little
girl. The people, including her own blood-related grandmother, became puzzling creatures for the girl, whose
actions drove her into a state of dread. Now there was not
the accustomed autumn chill but the icy atmosphere of
fear that penetrated little Tanya's heart.

Weeks and months went by. On each or almost each
Sunday the Baptist heresy was dinned into the little girl's
mind. Tanya grew used to the sensation of fear. She
watched when adults washed each other's feet for some
reason, and a look of puzzlement came over her face. She
noticed how they paid lip service in denouncing drunkenness, but at home, among guests they caroused. When she
was just about to ask a question, Granny carefully fore-
stalled it with a tender word:

"Everything's from God, honey."

Rumors about the abnormal way of life led by his
daughter reached Tanya's father, Vladimir Ovchinnikov,
foreman at the Khabarovsk Machine Tool-Building Plant.
And that Tanya's mother was not opposing it. When his ex-
wife died, he visited the grandmother and demanded Tanya.

"After the death of my daughter," rasped Evdokiya
Afanas'yevna in an ominous voice, "all that's hers—is
mine! Understand?"

Vladimir understood: Tanya had become a thing. And
then he decided to battle it out with the Baptist grandmother, and to snatch his daughter out of her grasp. He
sent off a declaration to the People's Court of the Rayon
imeni (named after) Lazo and asked that Tanya be given to

him for upbringing. The grandmother joined the battle and immediately switched over to the attack. She began to instill strongly into the grandchild that they wanted to "steal her, Tanya, and cut her up."

"Tanya, you have no papa. And this uncle who calls you his daughter is an Antichrist. He's thirsty for your blood. . . ."

When Vladimir Ovchinnikov arrived for a visit, Tanya fled from him as from the plague. She screamed:

"I'm scared, scared, scared!" and begged for someone to hide her.

Meanwhile the Court hearing dragged on. It was now this document that was not enough, now another. . . . Ovchinnikov sent off a letter to the editor. He mailed another to the Supreme Court.

Soon after this the trial was held. The People's Court, although delayed, did pass the correct decision: transfer Tanya to be brought up in her father's family.

It would appear that all points have been resolved. The little girl was wrenched out of the clutches of the Baptists. She is in school. She is under treatment. But I would like to continue the account.

Tanya has been enrolled in the Sita Primary School. Her teacher is Vera Petrovna Sinel'nikova, and she had been selected as part of the commission, preparing on request of the People's Court, the document of examination of the material status of E. A. Zabavina. The commission also included the former Rayon Inspector V. E. Bogoroditskaya and A. P. Nigey, deputy to the Sita Village Council.

Specifying in the document the farmstead plot of the Zabavinyye family, the home, and the size of the pensions, and recalling that E. A. Zabavina herself is a Baptist, the document compilers drew a strange conclusion, to put it mildly: "The school and the neighbors are against giving the child to her father. The girl must stay with her grandmother."

In the trial, schoolteacher V. P. Sinel'nikova was a witness and spoke in defense of the interests of the Baptist grandmother. This became the grounds for a particular finding by the Court in which it was stated that antireligious propaganda is poorly provided for in the Sita school.

I have not been able to meet with V. P. Sinel'nikova. She has worked in schools for a quarter of a century, mostly in Sita. She is no novice in teaching children. She has a good record in the public education division. And suddenly—this. Why?

"They (these Baptists)," explained Vera Petrovna, "are good people. They are against drunkenness. For friendliness . . . And that's why I tended to favor the grandmother. Also, I had heard many bad things about Tanya's father from her. I checked them. I see now that I made a mistake . ."

I met with teachers of the Sita Secondary School Young, perky, uncompromising. But a peaceful coexistence, so to speak, with the Baptists prevailed also in their case. "They don't seem to bother us."

"They don't bother us. . . ." Really! Sectarians work on the sly, and the Sita congregation, incidentally, has never been registered. Grief strikes a family. And here already someone of the "brother or sisters in Christ" has gone to the unfortunate one with their unctuous words, and picked off a victim. That is how it was with Sita resident, Istomina, a woman who was drawn into the sect. They know about this at the school. But none of the teachers waged a battle for the fate of a person.

We met with presbyter Chernolevskiy and with Zabavina. "Don't deceive your dear ones, is our first teaching," drawls one in a sing-song voice, and the grandmother seconds him. And she does deceive: "I did not lead the girl to the prayer meetings and she did not go there herself." Hemmed in by irrefutable evidence, the grandmother was compelled to tell the truth to the Court. But then she remarked to me: "What a fool I was, a fool. I should have taught the girl not to tell about this in the courtroom." "Does this mean teaching to deceive your dear ones?" I ask Zabavina. She is silent as the grave.

And one more fact compelled me to continue this conversation. Above I had referred to a particular finding of the Court. Unfortunately, it dealt only with case No. 2-624. The determination was not directed to the Rayon Public Education Division, nor to the Rayon Executive Committee.

. . . They say that a sacred place is never empty. Where the school and our ideology are not at work, others are. At times against us. Then what kind of peaceful coexistence with the Baptists are we talking about?

Sita-Khabarovsk
I. Grebtsov,
Our correspondent

EPILOGUE

Now that we have read these documents from the Soviet Press itself, what shall we say? We have read of Christians being sent to prison, and of children being taken from their parents. How should we react? Should we answer hatred with hatred?

Surely so! Hatred can be overcome by hatred only. Hatred is one of the Christian virtues. The first "gospel"— that given to Adam and Eve in the garden—talks of hatred when we read: "The Lord God said unto the serpent, Because thou hast done this, thou art cursed. . . . I will put enmity between thee and the woman" (Gen. 3:14, 15).

Jesus said, in the course of the Sermon on the Mount: "No man can serve two masters: for either he will hate the one and love the other . . ." (Matt. 6:24). Clearly Jesus considered hatred to be a necessary corollary to true love.

In the book of Revelation, our Master praises the Christians of Ephesus because they hated "the deeds of the Nicolaitanes, *which I also hate*" (Rev. 2:6, my italics).

To the hatred of the Communists we must answer with a still greater hate. But this hatred is not to be directed toward the men who do wrong. We must not hate the man, rather it is their hatred that we wish to hate and overcome. For the men themselves the fire we reserve must be the fire of love. They are but brothers in error who can and must be healed.

Once there was a great fire that broke out in a town. A man went to a burning house that was at the center of the blaze with a cup of water which he threw at the flames. Nothing happened; so he came back and said that water does not quench fire. Foolish man! A cup of water does not put out a fire, but rivers of water do.

The little love which we have cannot extinguish the fire of Communist hatred, but the rivers of living water that should flow from the heart of every Christian—these great streams can overcome hatred.

With about thirty other Christians I remember being in a prison cell in Rumania. One day the door was opened and a new prisoner was pushed in. It took us a little time to recognize him in the half-darkness of the cell. When we did recognize him we were amazed to see not a fellow Christian but a well-known Captain of the Secret Police who had arrested and tortured many of us. We asked him how he had come to be a fellow prisoner.

He told us that one day a soldier on duty had reported

that a twelve-year-old boy, carrying a pot of flowers, was asking to see him. The Captain was curious and allowed the boy to enter. When the boy entered he was very shy. "Comrade Captain," he said. "You are the one who arrested my father and mother, and today is my mother's birthday. It has always been my habit to buy her a pot of flowers on her birthday—but now, because of you, I have no mother to make happy."

"My mother is a Christian and she taught me that we must love our enemies and reward evil with good. As I no longer have a mother, I thought these flowers might make the mother of your children happy. Could you please give them to your wife?"

The Communist torturer is also a man. There is a chord in his heart that still vibrates at the word of truth and burning love. The Captain took the boy's flowers and embraced him with tears in his eyes. A process of remorse and conversion began. In his heart he could no longer bear to arrest innocent men. He could no longer inflict torture. In the end he had arrived with us in prison because he had become a defender of Christians.

Communists have killed our brethren and sisters, and continue to kill them. In Red China the churches have been closed and priests who persistently refused to deny Christ have been buried alive. Tens of thousands of Russian Christians have been arrested and Soviet prisons or asylums are full of them, even now.

Christians are tortured and held to ridicule before the public. They are shown as fanatics, obscurantists, illiterates, thieves and so on, but these charges reveal more about the characters of the accusers than of the accused. We who believe must surely feel compassion for men who can become so warped.

I hate this Communist hatred with all my heart; but I wish to overcome it by love.

From Church history we learn that, far from having resentment or bitterness, those who came out from Roman prisons in the first centuries were examples of understanding, love and tenderness. Tertullian, a Christian writer of the third century, says that those who endured tortures or imprisonment for their faith were considered to be so filled with the Spirit that they could absolve sins. More than that —they were prepared to forgive the gravest sins that no other Christian pastor of the day was prepared to overlook.

The result was that the Bishops were forced into opposing the "confessors" (as they were called) in this practice of absolution.

After the Decian persecution (250) thousands who had lapsed under pressure sought for restoration in the Church when the storm had subsided. Again it was those who had endured tortures for the sake of Christ who were the first to support a policy of forgiveness for the backsliders. One of the leading opponents of such a policy, Novatian, was a man who had never suffered himself and yet knew no forgiveness for those who had suffered and broken under the strain.

Christians come out from suffering more loving than they were before. They love their weaker brethren who could not suffer. They love even their torturers.

I cannot unite with what is called the "anti-Communist" fight in the vulgar sense of the word. Firstly because Communists are not the only persecutors of Christians. Our brethren are killed by Moslems in Nigeria and Sudan. I love these martyrs as much as the victims of Communism. Secondly, because I have learned from men of true wisdom that you can render a great service to mankind by remaining above the battle.

If I had lived in the times of the Reformation I think that I would have sided with Erasmus rather than with Luther. The latter asked for fire and a sword to uproot what was evil in the Roman Catholic Church. The result is that now, on the Continent at least, we have a Lutheran Church where many of its pastors believe in the Bible—so dear to Luther's heart—less than the Catholics of his day.

I prefer the battle to be in the sphere of ideas. Mankind goes toward physical suicide if it sets out to fight with nuclear weapons. Rather must error be fought by truth, and wrong opposed by righteousness. Without wanting to exclude violence in the self defense of the Christian civilization, my answer is love.

Would it be merely madness if thousands of Christians in London, Washington and the capitals of other nations were to take flowers to the Soviet Embassies and Consulates saying: "We love you even though you arrest, oppress, torture and kill our brothers. For the tears you bring us we bring you flowers"?

When the Russians entered Rumania they came looting, killing and raping. A Catholic priest in Galatz, a friend of mine, went to meet them with a plate of bread and salt, which was the traditional way of welcoming guests in a Rumanian home. He spoke the Russian language and approached them with words of love, and those words went home to their hearts. Many Rumanian Christians welcomed Russians to their homes. They were prayed for and many were secretly given gospels. We tried to be good to them, and many found Christ.

How would it be if, instead of answering the menace of Communism with the menace of nuclear war, we were to place our reliance on the word of truth and on deeds of love? Would this be madness? Christ was thought by some to be mad. So was St. Paul! Perhaps this sort of madness might prove to be the only remedy to the madness of Communist hatred. At least it would be a cheaper policy. The killing of every Vietcong costs £2,000, plus casualties, to the Americans. A gospel for him and a little food would cost much less.

These documents which I present will leave no room for doubt about the existence of a secret Underground Church in Russia. The same thing is true about other Communist countries. Why, then, are they not represented in the World Council of Churches or at the big Christian international conferences and conventions? Why do we in the West know nothing of their experiences?

Love, courage and heroism are contagious just as vice is contagious. As one man can learn drug addiction, alcoholism and other similarly wicked things from others, so we could learn much from these Soviet Saints! They sing a song we should learn. Behind the Iron Curtain, the Christian Church lives again in the heroic days of the first centuries.

It is said that during the Diocletian persecution in Rome (303) idols were placed throughout the city. Men had to worship them or die. The Bishop of Rome at the time recommended Christians to leave the city if they felt too weak to face martyrdom, rather than to stay in the city and commit idolatry. Among the Christians was a fifteen-year-old young aristocrat called Tiburtius. He went to the Bishop and said: "Is it not the first fruits that God asked from the Israelites? If some older folk take your advice and leave Rome, I will stay and offer God the flower of my youth." Tiburtius stayed in Rome, and he got the martyr's crown.

These documents have shown that in Russia today there are young people who are of the same breed as Tiburtius. These are youths prepared to resist openly the Communists, sacrificing their parental home, their careers, their liberties and their lives.

The Communists mock young Christians for spreading secret leaflets and singing hymns. St. Augustine said that whoever sang a hymn praised God twice because he praised God with the words and also in the music. Sometimes these young Soviet Christians have praised God three times. Their third form of praise has been their agonized cries under torture.

We are more powerful than the Communists. Greater courage and power is needed to face a whipping with a smile, than to do the whipping! Let them hate us; but we will love them. Love is a weapon that blesses the one who displays it and the other toward whom it is displayed. But this love should be balanced. Love obliges sometimes to violence toward those who endanger the triumph of love, as is the case with traitors in the Underground Church.

In the Communist camp, millions of our brethren have been killed, and continue to be killed and tortured. If these Christians had only thought about the immediate future they would have given up, but like Moses they considered the shame of the people of God to be of greater worth than the throne of Pharaoh. They looked to generations to come, and they kept the torch of Christianity burning in order to hand it to those who followed.

Jacob worked for Rachel for fourteen years and it seemed to him a little time because of his love for her. There is such comfort in the love which God has put in our little hearts, and more comfort still in the knowledge of His love for us. This comfort helps us to see the sufferings of this age to be of little importance. We read of one Tachenko saying "one night he heard a divine song from Heaven" (Article 19, p. 106). It might well have been—as the newspaper report suggested—a song that he had heard before. But this time it came from above.

I know from my own prison experiences, and from those of other Christians, that on sad Christmas Eves when we have suffered from the cold and hunger, and longed for our loved ones even more than usual, that we have been comforted by hearing the choirs of Heaven! We have known that the Angels were surrounding us just as certainly as when they appeared to the shepherds on the plains of Bethlehem. When you hear angelic songs, the brutal cries of the Communists don't count for so much.

We have tried to be fair and present reports not only of the Saints but also of the traitors who, for personal reasons, denied their Savior.

The Roman historian, Suetonius, tells the story of the emperor Caligula who began to rule his empire with high principles, but later abandoned them. After describing some of the good works of the early days, Suetonius wrote: "Thus are the deeds of the Prince among men; henceforth those of a veritable monster." We could say the same about our traitors. The prophet, Ezekiel, warned that if a man abandoned his righteous ways and began to sin—his former righteousness would be forgotten. These traitors have done us very great harm. In the matter of ruthlessness, they even surpassed the Communists on occasions.

But we continue to love them also, and we succeed to win some of them back to Christ. Others who cannot be regained must, I fear, receive their deserved punishment.

I have said, several times, that the situation in Russia and the Communist countries closely resembles that of the first centuries of Christian history. There is another side to this resemblance that I have not so far mentioned. Jewish Christians are playing a prominent role!

The first Christians were Jews. Jewish Apostles brought the Gospel to the other nations. "Has God rejected his people?" asked Paul the Apostle. "By no means" (Rom. 11:1, R.S.V.). The Apostle prophesied the return to Christ of a remnant of the Jews before the return of our Lord. And he was sure that this would mean great riches for the Gentiles.

Great personalities of the Jewish race in the West have declared themselves to be believers in Jesus—Albert Einstein, Henri Bergson, Nyils Bohr, Piccard, Franz Werfel, Shalom Ash and Martin Buber. In Russia and Rumania, Jewish believers play a most important role in the leadership of the Underground Church, and they number among the martyrs as in times of old. In the documents presented in this book we have come across the names of Grunvald, Hartfeld and others. These are Protestants. The Orthodox elements of the underground movement are led entirely by elements of the Jewish race, among them the priests, Eshliman and Yakunin, and the professor, Levitin. They were the first ones who had the courage to protest against the collaboration of traitors like the Patriarch Alexei and the Archbishop Nikodeme with the Communists.

In Rumania a Protestant pastor of Jewish origin, Milan Haimovici was one of the most respected sufferers for Christ. He spent many years in prison and under torture—but he was not broken!

One-third of the world's Jewry lives in the Communist camp. This should therefore form one-third of the concern, efforts and gifts of the Missions to the Jews. I study the magazines of many of these societies and happily, some have understood this to be their duty. It could not be otherwise.

Not to work toward winning these Jews for Christ means that evangelistic efforts in other parts of the world are very severely prejudiced. What would you think of a pastoral visit where one-third of the family were sick and the pastor did not even inquire about their health? American and British Jews have plenty of opportunities to hear the Gospel—Russian Jews have practically no such opportunities. Surely it is to these Jews in Communist lands that the missions must concentrate.

But if some Western missions to the Jews have failed, the Underground Church has not. It has won Jews for Christ, and these have become a great blessing for the Churches. They are very often the leaders. So God fulfills His ancient promise that Japheth (the European nations) will dwell in the tents of Shem (Gen. 9:27). Russians and Rumanians sit at the feet of Shem—of Hebrew Christians, and learn from them the word of God.

You see in this book the documents from the unknown world of the Underground Church—a Church of suffering, of fight and victory. Yes—of victory! Fifty years after the triumph of the Communist revolution in Russia *Komsomolskaia Pravda* writes: "In Krasnoiarsk, a city of half a million inhabitants, there is only one more or less active group of *Komsomol* members—atheists, consisting of fifteen students" (Article 13, p. 86).

Fifteen out of half a million after fifty years of intensive effort! That is *their* triumph! Those fifteen may terrorize. They may put Christians into prison. But they are still no more than fifteen!

May the readers of this book ask themselves how they can join hands with the Soviet Saints of the Underground

Church. We have read of Garbuzov being sentenced because he listened to "libelous programs from abroad" by means of radio (Article 9, p. 80). The Gospel, broadcast from the West, can be heard in Russia. The article entitled "Such Things Are Not Forgiven" deals with a girl who copied by hand pages from a Bible of Tsarist times. These Soviet Christians have practically no Bibles. You can send them! The Bibles sent in secretly do arrive. So do films, literature and tape recordings.

The hunger after the Word of God is great. On August 11, 1966, a hundred thousand copies of a selection of Old Testament stories were published under a name that disguised the contents. The publication was made possible through the combined efforts of members of the Underground Church who had attained high places in the State Publishing House at Moscow, and a Christian among the Communist censors. The news of the publication spread like fire and all the copies were sold in a matter of hours.

In 1967 a well-known denomination in Great Britain condemned in its annual report the activities of the European Christian Mission which brings Bibles secretly into Communist countries. There was, on the other hand, no condemnation or even mention of the killing of Christians in China, or the closing of Churches and callous imprisonment of believers in Communist countries. When British Christians protested at this and pointed out that Tyndale in Reformation times smuggled Bibles into Britain from the Netherlands, they got the answer that Tyndale had a right to do this because he was bringing them into his own country!

If that principle is to be taken seriously we may well ask if the Apostles were in the wrong! What right had they, as Jews, to bring the Gospel to Romans and Greeks? What right had the British to take the Bible to China and India? Why, then, should British people support the Bible Society which spreads the Word of God in 1,300 languages?

You do not ask the Devil if he permits the work of God! The Soviet Government forbids the spread of God's Word as the documents presented in this book make only too clear. Again foreigners are prohibited from bringing Bibles and Christian literature into the country. But why should we feel ourselves bound by the laws of an atheistic State?

Some of the most influential church leaders in England wrote to those who had inquired about these matters and said that it was the duty of Christians in Communist countries "to render to Caesar the things that are Caesar's." I disagree totally with this position. God is to be obeyed universally and unlimitedly upon the bare sight of His will. The laws of men, therefore, must be examined by the laws of God. If there is a clash between human and divine laws then we "ought to obey God rather than man" (Acts 5:29).

I appeal then to Western Christians—send Bibles and Christian literature to Communist countries. Keep broadcasting the Gospel in the languages of the Communist countries. And send practical aid to the families of Christian martyrs. All this, I know, will cost money, but then those who give their blood for the glory of God have a right to ask for money.

They have a right also to your concern and your love and your prayers. To give for this cause and be concerned may seem foolish to some, but just as the persecuted Christians in Russia look the most beautiful when they are mocked and put in their "dunces' caps" so perhaps the foolishness of Western Christians will reflect something of the same beauty in God's eyes.

A last question—what are the prospects for the immediate future? Will Communism mellow? Will it become softer on religion? Will the dunces' caps be taken off the heads of the Soviet Saints?

The answer is "No!" We see in Chinese and Albanian Communism the purest form of the creed. Other forms of Communism are likely to evolve in that direction, even if the paths taken by some of the countries may zigzag on the way. In Red China and Albania all the Churches have been closed. In China Christian prisoners have been terribly tortured.

We can be sure that this sort of development is likely, from the Bible. In the book of Revelation, chapter thirteen, we read that the beast will have power to overcome the saints. In the twelfth chapter of Daniel we read that "the power of the holy people" will be scattered.

Again common sense tells us not to trust in changes from people like the Communist rulers. In *King Lear* we read: "He's mad that trusts in the tameness of a wolf . . . or a whore's oath." Communists will not mellow but they do much to give this impression, and sadly some Christian leaders have forgotten Our Lord's warning to beware of wolves in sheep's clothing. Today we see this only too clearly. On the one hand the killing and torturing of Christians goes on at the hands of the Communists, and on the other hand they invite Christians of the West to friendly dialogue. They speak of friendly coexistence between the two ideologies but they do not practice it.

I once asked an important Communist leader what he understood by "friendly coexistence." In a moment of frankness he answered with a joke. "A hunter was about to kill a bear when the bear asked him why he wanted to do it. The hunter replied that he wanted the bear's fur. The bear replied: 'You must not take my life just for that! I'm ready to trade my fur for your rifle!' The hunter gave the rifle to the bear, and what followed is easy to guess."

The Church in Russia still survives by adapting herself to the necessities of Underground work. She even makes very encouraging progress. But the whole power of the State belongs to the Communists. At any time a new madman like Stalin could rise to kill millions of Christians and other innocent people. We have seen it in Red China.

We have to fight for the freedom of the Church behind the Iron Curtain. The inscription on the tomb of the Unknown Soldier in Westminster Abbey reads:

"He died for the freedom of the world"

If Christians in the West do not immediately come to the defense of their Russian brethren, then their fate will be similar to that of the Chinese and Albanian Churches.

But God does not sleep. In the end Communism will be conquered, although, I fear, much suffering lies ahead. How much, and how intense it will be, depends in great part upon the solidarity of the Western Christians with their persecuted brethren.

Some of the gloomy predictions of the Bible must not make us resign ourselves fatalistically to the extinction of the Churches in Communist countries. The book of Jonah shows with the repentance of Nineveh there exists also the possibility of God repenting of the evil He thought to do. If God changed His mind about destroying Nineveh, how much more can we hope for Him to change His mind when the fate of His faithful Church is at stake?

My book is finished. I have come through fourteen years of prison, hunger and doping. I write in what is a foreign language to me, and cannot express really what I think and feel. But I have done the best I can in this book to show the beauty of the Soviet Saints—the beauty of the bride of Christ adorned, by the Communists, with a dunce's cap.

Inquiries and gifts may be sent to

Jesus to the Communist World

P.O. Box 11, Glendale, California 91209

If you have enjoyed this book, you will want to read other inexpensive Pyramid best-sellers listed in the back of this book. You will find them wherever paperbacks are sold or you can order them direct from the publisher. *Yours For The Asking:* a free, illustrated catalogue listing more than 700 books published by Pyramid. Write the publisher: PYRAMID BOOKS, Dep't. K-99, 444 Madison Avenue, New York, N.Y. 10022.